Salted with Fire

Spirituality for the Faithjustice Journey

Fred Kammer, S.J.

PAULIST PRESS

New York/Mahwah, NJ

Robert Bolt, *A Man for All Seasons* (New York Vintage Books, 1962), p. 66.
Vintage Books is a subsidiary of Random House, Inc. Used with permission.

Cover Design by Robert Manning, Graphic Options, Hicksville, NY

Book design by Nighthawk Design

Library of Congress Cataloging-in-Publication Data

Kammer, Fred, 1945-
    Salted with fire : spirituality for the faithjustice journey / Fred Kammer.
        p.   cm.
    Includes bibliographical references and index.
    ISBN 0-8091-3540-X (pbk.)
    1. Christianity and justice—Catholic Church. 2. Sociology, Christian
(Catholic) 3. Church and social problems—Catholic Church. 4. Church work
with the poor—Catholic Church. 5. Catholic Church—Clergy—Religious life. I.
Title.
    BR115.J8K36 ~~1994~~ 1995   94-33444
    261.8—dc20   CIP

Published by Paulist Press
997 Macarthur Boulevard
Mahwah, New Jersey 07430

Printed and bound in the
United States of America

CONTENTS

To Pedro Arrupe, S.J., who inspired the service of faith and the promotion of justice among Jesuits, their colleagues in ministry, and many others across the world.

INTRODUCTION

Everyone must be salted with fire. Salt is good, but if salt becomes insipid, with what will you restore its flavor? Keep salt in yourselves and you will have peace with one another.

JESUS OF NAZARETH
MARK 9:49-50

This book is for the young who dream dreams of a more just world and their elders who see visions of peace. This book is for you who have had your hands dirtied, your mettle tested, and your hearts battered by working for a better world. This book is for you who have gone to bed distressed by the human suffering shown in the media and by what you have seen on the streets in your own community. This book is for you who have grown bone weary of fighting the good fight, want to collapse into a hammock by a mountain stream, and wish to God—and anyone else who will listen—that you did not care as much as you do.

For all of us concerned about children in poverty and hurting families, or about racial justice and stewardship of the environment, this book is about hope. What is offered here is not some naive hope that ignores the human suffering in our own country and across the world. Rather, this hope is wrapped in the awareness that new birth comes only after the pains of labor.

I write particularly for you who do the work of justice and peace from the base of your faith in God and in God's reign. As you know, in the midst of this work, you sometimes feel as if a compassionate God could not be more distant. Where is the God who extended a special concern for the **anawim**, the "little ones" among the Israelites, when 40,000 children worldwide die of hunger each day, when one-fourth of U.S. kids live in poverty, and when unborn children are aborted by the millions each year? Where is the God of Jesus, we ask, who identified himself in the 25th chapter of Matthew with the hungry, sick, and imprisoned, when millions are homeless in this rich nation, and food lines have replaced the family dining room for so many people?

1

Many of those who thirst for justice and work for peace have taken a real beating over the past fifteen years or more in this country. Their task has been made more difficult by the enormous cuts in federal and state spending on human services and social needs and by economic hard times. As just one example, Catholic Charities agencies nationwide reported that in 1992 74 percent of the persons who came to them for assistance needed the basic necessities of food and shelter; eleven years earlier this figure was only 26 percent. In some circles, it has even become fashionable to demean the poor and to despise those who work for and with them.

Three years ago, in **Doing Faithjustice**, I explored the connection between religious faith and social justice, tracing the dual Judaeo-Christian belief in Yahweh and in the preferential love of the poor from the pages of Genesis to the political realities of the late twentieth century. My hope in doing so was to animate faithful people to action for justice, and to give encouragement to those already involved in making the gospel take flesh in social, economic, and political fact. The religious and ethical tradition traced in that book and in the living faith written out in the lives of people who understand that tradition made it clear to me that faith and justice could not be separated. Their intimate connection defies efforts to make one concept prior to or instrumental to the other. The tradition, I argued, was best served by using the single word "**faithjustice**." I sought to promote the virtue of **faithjustice**, already vibrant in so many people, in these terms:

> **Faithjustice** is a passionate virtue which disposes citizens to become involved in the greater and lesser societies around themselves in order to create communities where human dignity is protected and enhanced, the gifts of creation are shared for the greatest good of all, and the poor are cared for with respect and a special love.

Faithjustice, I said, is a habit of the believing heart.

In this book, I want to move more deeply into the lived reality of **faithjustice** by exploring its impact on the lives of those who have taken up its challenge and survived the brutality that is poverty and the violence that hates reconciliation and peacemaking. In so doing, I will highlight some ways of hope for those already involved and for newcomers joining this pilgrimage.

The years have taught us many things that are shared when community organizers, Catholic Charities workers, political activists, and parish social ministers find the time to sit down and really talk. The political enthusiasms of the sixties and the social concerns of the post-

Vatican II church have matured in the harsh sun of the seventies, eighties, and now nineties.

We who have worked for justice and peace have endured the departures of many companions from our journey with the poor. We have encountered a political intolerance fashionable among some of the privileged and powerful, and seen budget cuts and tax packages that further enriched the wealthy and impoverished the poor. As people of faith, we were both encouraged by the new volunteers joining in our efforts to respond to the poor, and grieved by the religious avoidance too common among other churchgoers.

But, as faithful and persistent people, we also dreamed dreams and learned lessons which have enriched our lives, fired our hearts, and healed our wounds. We have been schooled by the desert and the kindness of prayer, by the tears and laughter of companions along the way, by arduous and sometime lonely labors, and by the good and evil of the poor themselves. It is from these companions inside and outside the churches and from others who stopped along the way that I have tried to gather this book.

Introduction to the Pastoral Circle

This book focuses on the topic of a spirituality of social ministry or social activism through a number of different perspectives. They are organized or mediated through the matrix of what Joe Holland and Peter Henriot of the Center of Concern[1] call the Pastoral Circle. Underlying this approach are several preliminary observations which I would like to discuss. First is the observation of what we all know, that the macrosystems—and many microsystems—are not working well. A world in which tens of thousands of children die each day of poverty and malnutrition is not in very good shape. We have schools that do not teach, politicians who do not govern, banks that do not lend, prisons that do not rehabilitate, and economic systems that widen the gap between rich and poor individuals and nations.[2]

The second observation, reflecting on such diverse social structures as neighborhood organizations, families, international entities, and interpersonal relations, is that all of these entities tend to become self-protective. They instinctively fend off most criticism and any significant proposed change. This is even true for those who are committed to work for social change and the agencies through which they work.

Obviously, there is a positive side to this defensiveness in that we need our institutions and structures to be self-sustaining. We humans need consistency in those ways of behavior which we have found to be good and helpful. Nevertheless, there is an inbuilt stagnation in all of those ways we have of doing what we do, a tendency not to change nor to adapt to changing circumstances nor to the changing populations which institutions serve. In failing to so adapt, those structures or organizations often become divorced from their original purposes.

A classic example occurs in those congregations of sisters, brothers, or priests who say, "Our religious community began by teaching; and our constitutions say that we teach poor, immigrant children." Now, however, with powerful U.S. cultural assimilation, these same religious congregations find themselves teaching the upper-middle-class suburban heirs of four-generations-bygone immigrant children. Joseph Daoust calls this "ministerial bracket creep."[3] Not that teaching suburban youth is not valuable work or ministry, but the original purpose of the religious community seems to have been lost. Many religious now find themselves saying, prompted by Vatican II's call to renewal, "Well, wait a minute; what was our original purpose, our charism? We want to go back to that charism."

The point of this example is that any group, no matter how well-intentioned, can become easily divorced from its original purposes. This occurs by accident, secondary results of chosen courses of conduct, or design. This is true of many structures, organizations, and activities in fields as varied as education, politics, and health care. Even people who altruistically set out to serve others in the private, non-profit sector often find this to be the case. It is an awareness that comes painfully.

Because of this phenomenon common to governments, government programs, human service institutions, and churches, there has evolved in the last twenty years an approach to criticizing, on an ongoing basis, the activities, structures, and organizations in which we all are engaged. Henriot and Holland capture this methodology in what they call the Pastoral Circle, consisting of four "mediations of experience."

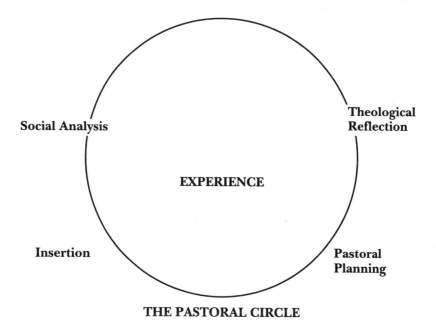

Social Analysis

Theological Reflection

EXPERIENCE

Insertion

Pastoral Planning

THE PASTORAL CIRCLE

In their words:

> This circle is frequently referred to as the "circle of praxis," because it emphasizes the on-going relationship between reflection and action. (The concept of **praxis** has been developed by Paulo Freire in his classic, *The Pedagogy of the Oppressed*, New York: Herder and Herder, 1970.) It is related to what has been called the "hermeneutic circle," or the method of interpretation that sees new questions continually raised to challenge older theories by the force of new situations.[4]

Four phases or moments characterize this critical method: insertion, social analysis, theological reflection, and pastoral planning. The first aspect was initially called **experience**, and is now dubbed **insertion**. Here we reflect upon the wealth of experience which we have of the social, cultural, economic, and political reality. This is not the stuff of books and lectures, but of felt experience. The privileged Christian prism is the experience of the poor themselves and of those standing with, taking sides with, and in solidarity with the poor.

The next moment in this process is called **social analysis**, the more technical process which is intimately linked with **theological reflection** in the hands of the religious person. Such analysis is seldom value-free, even among those engaged in what passes for the social sciences in our civil society.

The third phase of this approach to social reality is **theological reflection**, in which we bring to bear on what is analyzed the values rooted in scripture, theology, and our lived faith. Here we are often judging what we have perceived from our experience and subsequently analyzed.

Finally, under the heading of **pastoral planning**, experience, analysis, and reflection converge in the decision-making process, choosing a course of action for the present and future. That action (or inaction), in turn, creates or leads us into a new set of experiences which themselves should give rise to new analysis, valuing, and decisions... and so forth—thus the circle.

One critical reason for promoting the Pastoral Circle has been to try to preempt the assumptions about institutions, people, and courses of action that are so often identified with ideologies. Anthony Tambasco explains:

> Sociology of knowledge warns us not only that presuppositions influence the ways in which we view reality, but also that our presuppositions can often prevent our coming to an accurate view of reality at all. Liberation theologians have spoken frequently of this problem as a problem of ideology, stressing its importance especially on the political or economic level. There is a strong tendency for those in power to hold tenaciously to a view of things which enables them to justify (above all to themselves) keeping the poor in oppression. Ideology can be defined as a predisposition to see things in a certain way, operating prior even to conscious reasoning, which makes it difficult if not impossible to see things clearly.[5]

Religion and theology are key players in this concept of ideology, often reinforcing the blindness which serves economic and political power. Ideology then plays a "legitimating function" which is "deeply embedded, all-pervading, and difficult to combat."[6] The Pastoral Circle approach was designed to promote action based upon actual experience, mediated through analysis of the situation, reflection from a faith perspective, and decisions and action which produce new experiences.

The circle thus becomes a method of an ongoing critique of any action. In simple terms, it says, this is not working as well as we originally thought it would. This organization is not accomplishing what it set out to do. Maybe we need to look again at this situation, analyze what we are doing and the values we want to pursue, and restructure what we are working on. The new course of action may be radically different, or just fine-tuning. That action in turn becomes new experience which we analyze, reflect upon, and modify again, thus creating still more new experiences.

The Pastoral Circle should help us make better decisions about our actions. We are encouraged to avoid the pitfalls of ideology which can lock us into the paralysis of, "That's the way we do it here." Note, however, that each moment in the process can also be subject to ideological or other narrowness. For example, we may only experience our own kind of people. We may analyze only from one methodology. We may reflect out of one school of thought. Finally, we may decide upon a course of action limited by predetermined options. Each moment of the circle, then, must itself be subject to ongoing scrutiny.

This approach also directly responds to the fact that structures, organizations, and systems become self-protective, stagnate, and often lose their sense of original purpose. This is true of marriages, universities, non-profit associations, and churches themselves. For those working for a more just and compassionate society, though, the Pastoral Circle is particularly applicable to those institutions and structures which either create or reinforce social injustice.

In this book, moreover, I use the circle in two different ways. First, I have organized the material of the four chapters around the four "mediations of experience" in order to deepen our appreciation of each. More precisely, chapter one begins in the darkness of forms of burnout, experiences too familiar to many people engaged in social service or social change work. In chapter two, we then look directly at social analysis, both the reasons for doing it and a kind of "how to" approach to the subject for the activist. Then, in chapter three, we move from an exercise in the kind of social and cultural analysis described in chapter two to theological reflection upon personal, communal and social injustice and its implications for those involved in social justice work. Finally, chapter four explores the ways of living that have sustained the past and present in social ministry and suggests hope-filled paths into the future.

My second use of the Pastoral Circle is built upon a recurring and overlapping approach to its very structure, one which I hope the authors would find congenial. True, the chapters in turn do focus on insertion, analysis, theological reflection, and proposals for action. They do so, however, in a way that involves all four moments, at least implicitly, in every chapter. Rather than take a single question or specific issue through all four moments of the process of the circle, I have chosen to concentrate primarily on the broad topic of social ministry or social action itself. Because of this breadth, each chapter looks at different aspects of this kind of work, not as different moments in a single effort, but more as waves rolling upon a beach. Each wave does build upon the preceding ones, but with different peaks and troughs emphasizing different aspects of this ministry. This design is required by the broad purposes of deepening our understanding of what social action is and learning how it might be done more effectively in the future. This is, in the truest sense, spirituality done "outdoors" in the world in which God is ever present and ever active.

Spirituality is essentially about seeing God's presence and activity in the midst of human reality. In a way, we look through or past the apparent object and event and see its inner self, trying to discern the movements of God's grace and the opposing forces of evil, their interplay, and our own roles in the conflict. Thus, spirituality, rather than some purely personal combination of faith and feelings, is enriched and made more honest by the insights of the various social sciences. It insists on seeing reality in its social or structural manifestations which reveal the three-dimensional depth of all our relationships, including our relationship to God. Just as psychology has influenced our understanding of spirituality over the past thirty years, so it is now time for social intuition and insight to help us to better see the fully complex truth of ourselves in our relationship to others and to God.

As each chapter opens, I offer several brief personal vignettes from legal services, Catholic Charities, or Catholic social justice work—mostly in the South—only to set the scene for more in-depth consideration in the material which follows. Sometimes the vignettes are referred to specifically later in the chapter, but mostly they are suggestive of the contents and approach.

My desires are several. For newcomers, I wish you hope and courage in going forward in the service of justice and peace with your eyes more open to the challenges ahead and with some new provisions for your journey. For those who have been on the road for years, I hope that, in reading this book, you will recall your own lessons in living **faithjustice**, renew your memories of the heroines and heroes of your own pilgrimage, and explore more profoundly the depths of your connectedness to God and to God's own poor. Those efforts hopefully will refire your passion and renew your commitments. They will make you a source of strength and encouragement for others with whom you live and work.

My gratitude to the Society of Jesus: to the New Orleans Province, the Woodstock Theological Center at Georgetown University, and the

Woodstock Jesuit Community for ideas, insights, and time and a place to write. My thanks to the K. Street Jesuit Community, where I live in the District of Columbia, for patience, support, and living with our faces turned toward the world. My special appreciation for review and suggested revisions of manuscript drafts to Ed and Marybelle Hardin, Betsy Hartson, R.S.C.J., Kate Haser, Phil Land, S.J., Jonathan Montaldo, John Kavanaugh, S.J., Jim Martin, Dick Sparks, C.S.P., and Kitty Wach. I especially want to thank the men and women of the Jesuit National Social Ministries Board and Office for being a community of dialogue for me in the late seventies and early eighties, searching for the connections between how we live, what we work for, and how God moves in our world and in ourselves.

CHAPTER ONE

From Compassion Fatigue to Burnout

The world will not be changed, poor people will not receive their basic rights, militarism will not be stopped, trust will not be built between nations, justice will not arrive if tired, bleary eyed, depressed, burnt-out people are those trying to bring about change....Coming from a tradition of martyrs, I feel particularly tempted to be a martyr for the poor, for my work, for my faith. This is not to say that we are never called to self-sacrifice and even death, but I do believe no one has ever been called to burn themselves out.

J ODY S HEARER
MENNONITE ACTIVIST[1]

During the height of the tensions in Mobile after Dr. King's assassination, two Quaker community organizers addressed the students gathered in an auditorium on the campus of Spring Hill College. They prodded us to become involved full-time in working for racial and social justice, arguing that pursuing higher studies was a luxury that America in the sixties could not afford. If we did not solve the race problem now, they urged, it would be too late.

* * *

At a 1977 meeting of Jesuits involved in social ministries in the Maryland Province, the discussion turned to the question of how to deal with frustration and guilt that often attend the failures they experienced in their work. The well-known Father Horace McKenna, himself an elder veteran of years of commitment to the poor in Washington, D.C., rose to his feet and declared, "I don't get frustrated; I JUST GET MAD!"[2]

* * *

In 1977, Dick Smith, a friend who had worked as a community organizer in Oakland, California, wrote:

> *I recall that when I arrived in Chicago a few years ago to receive some initial training in community organizing, the instructor explained to us that a sense of anger and of rage was a sine qua non of a good organizer. If you were inca-*

11

*pable of anger, you were likewise incapable of organizing. Saul Alinsky himself,
the belated godfather of community organizing in this country, used to say that
an organizer, while burning against injustice, must also know how to "bridle
his anger so that it becomes cold and hard. Then he acts with calculation." The
point I make in citing these two men is this: Anger is a necessary motivation for
anyone passionately concerned about justice....Yet it is also recognized that it
must be bridled and channeled so that it doesn't devour either the individual
himself or those for whom he must be a friend and a brother. The goal of a good
organizer is not to make enemies but to repair a situation of injustice–and that
effort will more often than not require that one become enraged at those responsible for the injustice.*[3]

* * *

*In each of the budgets he submitted to Congress during his two terms,
President Reagan "zeroed out" the Legal Services Corporation (LSC), which
funded civil legal services for low-income people. Legal services programs, especially California Rural Legal Assistance Corporation, had earned Reagan's
lasting enmity during his governorship of California. They had shown the
temerity to sue Governor Reagan and the State of California on behalf of farm-
workers, consumers, welfare mothers, and a wide range of other low-income citizens who disagreed with or were injured or threatened by actions of the state.*

*While Congress would never let LSC be defunded, it allowed LSC funding
to be cut 25 percent during the first Reagan year and to remain substantially
frozen since then. More critically, however, the administration, its congression-
al supporters, and Reagan appointees to the LSC Board of Directors carried
out an ongoing campaign to undercut legal services for the poor. They tried to
strip away from LSC funded programs and from poor clients their access to
class actions, appeals, representation of their organizations and associations,
lawsuits that generated attorneys fees, legal resource centers, and resort to reg-
ulatory reform or state legislatures or Congress to redress their injuries or pursue their interests. No one yet has documented the immense costs which were
experienced among the women and men who comprise the staffs, boards, and
volunteers of legal services programs. Nor have they measured the impact of
this unrelenting attack on the ability of programs to represent clients.*

*While the "war on poverty" had been widely criticized by Reagan and con-
servatives for its alleged ineffectiveness, those in legal services component of
that war felt that they were assaulted repeatedly because they had been too
effective. Their sense of irony deepened when President Bush blamed the same
war on poverty for the 1992 Los Angeles riots.*

Why is it that activists in social ministry seem to have the longevity
of members of a bomb squad? Why is it that brevity seems to be the

one common characteristic of a wide variety of forms of work for social change or in direct contact with the poor and their problems? Some commentators speak of compassion fatigue among caring professionals in increasingly stressful work.[4] Others point to a more extreme condition of burnout, the focus of this first chapter. The word "burnout" refers to a physical, emotional, psychological, and spiritual phenomenon. Burnout is an experience of personal fatigue, alienation, depression, failure, and more that seems characteristic of the lives of a number of social activists.[5]

This burnout phenomenon has a varied impact on activists. After only a few years of direct ministry, they may move to managing or training others, to graduate studies, or to some other work. They may drop out of social ministry and a religious community or their church at the same time. Perhaps, worst of all, they may remain in social ministry long after their usefulness, creativity, and caring have ended. The signs of burnout are evident when clients become "caseloads," people become "issues," and the activist becomes a bureaucratic functionary or worse.

This phenomenon is not unique to religiously motivated activists. In a ground-breaking 1976 study, researchers at the University of California at Berkeley examined burnout as a phenomenon common to many health and social-service professionals: poverty lawyers, physicians, prison personnel, social-welfare workers, clinical psychologists in mental hospitals, child-care workers, and psychiatric nurses. The California study described the effect of burnout as a loss of emotional feeling for the persons they are working with, treatment of clients or patients in detached or dehumanized fashion, distancing by the worker as a way of coping with stress, and eventual resignation from the job. Along the way, the workers often develop cynical and negative feelings about their clients or patients, and begin to treat them as numbers or files.[6]

Numerous conversations and discussions over the years since 1976 have confirmed for me the problem of burnout for social activists. While there is not as much explicit talk about burnout as there was ten or fifteen years ago, the experience continues among people I personally know: social workers; legal services personnel; Catholic Charities staffers; parish social ministry volunteers; and cause-advocates. When they hear a list of symptoms of burnout, their heads nod knowingly.

Many professionals have discussed burnout primarily in terms of personal factors, but more recent analysis has been conducted in organizational and environmental terms. Both kinds of factors are presented in this chapter.

The personal experience of burnout is described poetically as, "Burnout is the 'morning after' of commitment," and "Burnout is what happens when we near the end of the short wick of our commitment candle."[7] More analytically, however, burnout has been described empirically as follows:

> Burnout is a syndrome of emotional exhaustion, depersonalization, and reduced personal accomplishment that can occur among individuals who work with people in some capacity. Emotional exhaustion refers to feelings of being emotionally overextended and drained by one's contact with other people. Depersonalization refers to an unfeeling and callous response toward these people, who are usually the recipients of one's service or care. Reduced personal accomplishment refers to a decline in one's feelings of competence and successful achievement in one's work with people.[8]

Key to this development in burned-out individuals is the loss of the sense of mission which first brought them into the work of social justice.[9] This loss of vision and commitment also is the key distinction between burnout and the problems of stress or workaholism.

As a personal process, burnout seems to pass through three levels of intensity. The first is characterized by signs and symptoms which are relatively mild and short in duration, often treatable with a short break or diversion. Level two is characterized by more stable and lasting symptoms and requires a more extraordinary response, such as a long weekend away. The third level is seen in chronic symptoms, accompanied by a physical or psychological illness such as an ulcer, hypertension, or depression. Outside intervention is usually needed.[10]

In another analysis, three stages of personal burnout are characterized, first by physical warning signs (persistent colds, headaches), then by emotional and behavioral symptoms (angry outbursts, irritability), and finally by **terminal burnout**. This terminal condition is marked by sourness about others and oneself, intense loneliness, and alienation.[11] A long list of signs and symptoms have appeared in the literature as well.[12]

People of faith should recognize the existence of this problem, especially since the **faithjustice** call to the churches in the late twentieth century implies a more extensive commitment of personnel in the direction of active involvement with the poor and the problems of the poor. Moreover, the social activists' burnout problem raises issues that touch every believer, in social ministry or not. In personal spiritual terms, there are problems concerning anger, frustration, hostility, and potential failure. Questions in the sphere of ministry arise about the exercise of power, the use of conflict, and the need for competence. Christian worldview concerns involve the permanent presence of evil in human society, a certain naiveté in both pragmatic political analysis and faith-vision, and the constant contrast between idealistic hopes and realistic possibilities for change agents. Finally, the integrity of the faith community itself is threatened by themes of alienation, identity, and disunity. The issues involved in the burnout discussion which follows have echoes in every form of contemporary ministry.

This chapter examines and reflects on this problem with both descriptive and analytical materials. Its scope encompasses psychological, spiritual, social, ministerial, and political dimensions precluding any definitive solution. Rather, my hope is that this presentation of the burnout experience and some suggestions about lines of response will contribute to ongoing work of many commentators from different disciplines. It may also help activists to fashion their own ways of coping successfully. In chapters three and four, we will return to themes from this chapter and to ways of survival in the face of the variety of complex and powerful forces involved.

Significant Strains Associated with the Work

Many social activists seem chronically tired, frustrated, and overextended. Why? There are a number of factors which produce these reactions, and which interplay to aggravate the condition. The first set of these factors arises from the work of social service or social change and from the impact of this work upon the persons involved, their worldview, and their relations to others inside and outside their work experiences. They begin with experiences of failure, personal imperative, structural awareness, and anger.

When Father Pedro Arrupe, Superior General of the Jesuits, met with the Jesuit province Directors of Social Ministries in St. Louis in December, 1975, he first listened intently and sympathetically to a series of regional reports, plans, and agenda for social ministry. Then he shocked the group by assuring the activists that, despite their wonderful efforts and even more imaginative dreams, all their efforts would fail.

Arrupe was speaking from a particular theological worldview rooted deeply in the gospels. He saw failure as an intrinsic part of all efforts to effect societal change and build up the reign of God. The view is integral to many forms of spirituality which stress the experience of compassion and companionship with the suffering Christ.[13] Moreover, Arrupe was describing a factual, everyday experience of many activists. As one ex-organizer told me, "Everything I touched turned to failure."

For some in ministry, the sense of failure and the strain of their work may be attributed to the kinds of persons with whom they work. These may be the hard cases of those street people who suffer from a complex of difficult personal, medical, social, and psychological problems. Stress may be more acute in working with persons with HIV/AIDS, too. Special concerns for AIDS workers arise from the complex clinical course of the disease, its psychosocial implications, the necessity of confronting values and attitudes, the increase in caseloads, dwindling resources, and the inevitability of grief and loss.[14] Similar special stresses have been attributed to persons who care for the elderly. These workers carry both the ordinary burdens of health care professionals and the additional burdens of dependency, loss, and depression related to the aging process.[15]

For those at the grassroots, direct-ministry-to-basic-needs level, a palpable sense of failure also arises from the sheer massiveness of the problem. For every ten people they help or work with, there seem to be a thousand more. At food pantries, homeless shelters, and legal services offices, the same problems appear day after day seemingly without relief. Things are not, after all, getting better and better, says this experience. Of course, governmental studies have indicated repeatedly that the poor are in fact getting poorer in relation to the prosperity of the rest of the country, the cost of living, and their share of social goods. A common response is to dig in deeper and become more involved, with too much to do and not enough time to do it in. This can cause a bone-deep personal fatigue.

This digging-in, in turn, is related to an unrelenting sense of personal imperative about the work of social justice and the needs of the poor. This was the case in Mobile in the late sixties when the Quaker neighborhood workers made their impassioned plea to students at Spring Hill College to drop out of college and hit the streets. They insisted that unless something was done about poverty and racism "immediately," it would be too late.

In part, this experience of urgency is due to the high ideals and motivation of many people who enter various service professions or commit themselves to social ministry.

> Workers most susceptible to burnout are usually highly motivated, perceptive, caring, and action oriented, with high expectations of them-

selves and others. Often such persons will push themselves beyond healthy limits in attempts to meet their unrealistically high standards of care and personal goals. Over time, as they discover that their best efforts are not working, they can become disillusioned and confused. When distress accumulates without relief, some unpleasant consequences can emerge.[16]

Rather than high ideals, other observers suggest that a Messiah complex lies at the heart of this imperative, that activists believe that if they themselves do not get things done, no one will. Still others argue that guilt is the driving motivation, since many activists come largely from middle-class and well-to-do backgrounds, the "haves" of American society. To the contrary, some activists attribute this condition, not to their own characteristics, but to the overwhelming needs of the poor and their acute pain at the hands of the larger society. As one community organizer expressed it, "I hate it; it's the worst work I've ever done. But my faith calls me to it."

Work at the people-and-needs level may also awaken what one Mexican calls "structural utopian awareness."[17] This is the consciousness which arises out of contact with the mass of individual problems and which affirms that there really are structural and systemic causes of the problems of everyday life among the poor and that "the system's got to change." A good statement of this appeared from an activist in Appalachia:

> We wasted time out here for a couple of years setting up community centers, repairing schoolhouses, providing fun and games for the youngsters, and summer programs—all of which were incidental to the main concern...A life-and-death struggle is going on over strip mining here that can spell doom to the future of this area. The only way to end it is to organize people, to get them together to voice their demands.[18]

This kind of consciousness brings with it sharp dissatisfaction with work designed more to meet immediate needs than to change societal structures; and for those doing such work it is a part of the experience of failure described above.[19]

Even if one is working at the structural and systemic level, however, failure can be a constant companion. "The system" often is like the mythical dragon—cut off a head and two grow back. Work hard to change some aspect of the political, financial, or legal structures of a city, for instance, and some new means of enslavement will be devised. This was part of our experience as consumer lawyers in Georgia where years of painstaking litigation on behalf of poor buyers and borrowers were nullified in a single session of the Georgia Legislature in the eighties.

The more knowledgeable activists become, the more pervasive and powerful do the "sinful social structures"[20] appear. In addition, if activists work at this structural level for too long, they may find themselves out of touch with the people they intended to serve or the problems they set out to remedy. This too causes frustration and failure. These in turn give rise to pain and anger, and thence to blame, hostility, guilt, and a range of other powerful emotions.

One prominent superior in a religious congregation argued that many members of his congregation involved in direct social action in the sixties and seventies were working out inappropriate anger and authority hang-ups. One sympathetic non-activist, who lived with a Midwest religious community composed primarily of community organizers, put it this way, "They had to have an other, and they extended the conflict model even to dealings with their own religious superiors." Similar feelings have been acknowledged by people active in social ministry.[21] These observations suggest that attitudes of anger and hostility exist for some activists before going into the work of social change and even affect their choice of this work.

Some activists respond that anger results from involvement in the work of social justice, not vice-versa. Situations of injustice and poverty simply draw out the anger and anti-authoritarian elements that are present in most people. More people would share their anger, activists say, if they were exposed to the experience of the poor, if they had their own "consciousness raised." Activists find support for this among those psychologists who hold that one of the natural causes of anger is the perception of injustice to oneself or others.[22]

Anger, then, may be a normal, not abnormal, response to these experiences of injustice. Managing the anger and even rage that injustice can produce, however, requires a deep understanding of its causes and how the anger operates within each of us. It also calls for learning positive responses to keep these feelings from becoming self-destructive.[23] Some connect the anger of the activist to God's own anger at the outrage of human injustice. Others distinguish the structural injustices from personal sin so to be better able to forgive other persons.[24] Still others focus on the development of personal habits such as deep breathing, jogging, and other forms of exercise to relieve stress and tension created by anger. These are complemented by recommendations for talking with support groups, appropriately trained professionals, or even friends about anger-producing situations, new ways of feeling and thinking, channeling the energy of anger into creative responses, and practicing the familiar virtue of forgiveness.[25] *[More on anger in chapter four.]*

Many of the pressures experienced by activists are situational or social, for example, violence, the style of their work, closing circles of friends and contacts, and the absence of role models. It is commonplace to refer to the **general violence** imposed by "the system" upon the poor, that which tears up families and destroys bodies, mind, and spirits. Watchers of TV news are also familiar with the current of **actual physical violence** that flows swiftly through the ghettoes and slums of urban and rural America. Recent riots in Los Angeles and elsewhere are only the most recent reminders of this fact. This violence is also part of the world of many social activists. A significant number of activists can recite tales of actual violence and fear of violence in their lives: the bomb thrown through the legal-aid office window, dark streets and darker public-housing corridors, civil-rights marches, physical threats, and death itself. As one activist put it, "I got burned; I saw a friend of mine killed. The enemy struck back at us." This condition of violence is absent from the lives and work of many other religious people and from the social activist's own prior work. It adds personal fear and fear for fellow workers and the poor to an already difficult task. Finally, when activists see their own efforts as somehow responsible for violence or violent death, this perception greatly complicates their situation with guilt and related emotions.

Another disconcerting factor for activists may be the particular style of their work. Its structure is the first of several aspects of this problem. Unlike much work in traditional jobs or in some institutions such as schools or hospitals, the activist's job is often unstructured, flexible, and self-starting. Besides making personal life irregular and sometimes disjointed, the lack of structure complicates the possibilities of family life or religious community. Family and community meals, days off, visiting with friends, prayer, vacations, and even simple relaxation fall victim to the erratic pace. Efforts to put structure into one's personal, family, or community life may be resisted as either artificial or unsympathetic to the needs of those served. After all, how can I take a regular day off when so many people are hungry, homeless, or suffering?

A further aspect of the style problem was suggested in a meeting of community organizers in the Midwest. At that meeting they referred to the "lead organizer style," marked by strong language, heavy smoking, long meetings, heavy drinking, and late hours. The same might be said of other social activists for whom the pace is fast, competition is woven throughout their day, and conflict is a major theme. This style is an exhausting one for anyone, even more so for new people breaking into a work, for whom style and substance often are difficult to distinguish.

A curious aspect of style is the often cluttered and dirty environs of the activist, at home or at work. Whether this is the result of shoestring budgets, a countercultural reaction to middle-class values, or being too busy to clean up, dirt and clutter abound. This scene prompts at least two reactions. One is the increased tension and frustration of the work itself, adding to unstructured schedules and incessant client demands. The other response is an unwillingness of others in other ministries to work or live with some social activists.

In general, many activists find the circle of their social contacts and friends becoming increasingly narrow over time. Those with whom they grew up or attended school seem a long way from the inner city or the migrant camp. The poor with whom they work often do not accept them on a social basis—due to such differences as race, class, and education. Eventually, cut off from their past and isolated in the present, activists may spend both their on-duty and leisure time mostly with other activists.

This narrowing circle of friends could be due to ordinary human patterns of interaction in the United States, which are now more related to job or lifestyle than neighborhood or family.[26] The activist's relative isolation, however, also may result from a kind of siege mentality growing out of alienation from others or from a pervasive fatigue that inhibits development of hobbies, new friends, vacations, reading, professional development, and sometimes a sense of humor. Some may also be affected by a kind of self-righteousness that devalues other kinds of work or ministry. Fewer available friends in turn intensifies the personal anguish and loneliness produced by the job and social reality. The isolation also can inhibit a broadening of horizons that would help the activist work more productively and creatively. This isolating phenomenon can also affect activists who are married and their spouses. As one person observed to me, "Of all the activists of the sixties whom I knew, none of their marriages survived."

Many contemporary branches of social activism are relatively new. Legal services, community organizing, VISTA, parish social ministry, Peace Corps, community action programs, and the environmental movement, all are creations of the second half of the twentieth century, at least in their contemporary form. As a result, all have two elements in common: the vast majority of those involved have been young people;

and they had few models or mentors to show them how to do what they were undertaking. They also had few models for long-term commitment to the work into which they entered, commitment that would last through marriage, child-rearing, middle age, and seniority.

In many religious congregations of women and men, by contrast, there was a long tradition of members committed to service of the poor and to working for social change. These pioneers of earlier generations, however, were seen as rugged individualists by some, and mavericks and loners by others. Some were this way by choice or personality or work schedule. Others became loners because their communities resented and resisted their work. Some were proclaimed as great women and men and were hailed, late in life, as great members of their religious families. They often appear unique and inimitable.

One result of this heroic stature is that there are few viable models for younger members of the congregation to imitate and build upon. There are even fewer community-team models. This is a critical factor when increasing numbers of younger religious have entered social ministry or expressed a desire to do so. Without effective models, individual or team ministry and community or personal lifestyle become unknowns, new challenges, and complicated ventures. These religious then share the condition of many of their lay contemporaries in lacking models for long-term commitment.

For laypeople carving out their way in the thickets of social ministry within the church, the problem of effective models is often aggravated by the elevation of priests and religious to the status of social justice saints. There are far too few lay models of effective social ministry held up within the church community. In one inner-city parish, for example, the pastor uses his heroic priest predecessor as a model of social concern in his homilies. He fails to realize that the pattern of full-time, ordained, celibate ministry—inspiring for his own dedicated labors—is not well suited to the lives of married, employed, child-raising lay adults. The absence of such models also is criticized as **the Ralph Nader Syndrome**, where the glorification of Nader's monastic life, meager income, 400-plus hours of monthly work, and austere lifestyle set a "warped and inhumane standard" for aspirants to public interest careers.[27]

The absence of models also complicates training, since one of the primary modes of training in many professions and in many religious congregations is an internship. The neophyte is placed in an office, school, or hospital to learn while working, by doing a job under the watchful eye of a veteran. In religious congregations, newcomers also learned from living with others who had chosen teaching or hospitals as their ministry.[28] Until there are a sufficient number of people in social ministry to provide models for younger persons and situations for community and training, those entering this work do so without a powerful aid available in other fields. The same challenge faces those who look for models of happily married activists to provide both assurance that marriage and social ministry are compatible and ways of successfully blending the two.

Another important factor affecting entry into many areas of social change work is finances. The activist is often concerned not only for his or her living expenses but also for the cost of any programs to be initiated. The further he or she moves from traditional occupations for which a decent salary might be available from church or private or public agency, the harder it is to find supporting resources and the more time must be expended in fund-raising. This, too, strains the activist, especially those contemplating marriage and child-rearing.

The occasion for burnout comes when the aggravating realities associated with the work itself—community, environment, the pain of the poor, overextension, style, fatigue, loneliness—run headlong into the consciousness of the enormity and complexity of the task of creating a better society or of providing any lasting assistance to needy people. Activists may be only vaguely aware of the factors clashing within them. The impact, however, can destroy the validity of everything they are doing and the viability of work for social change itself.

Alienation from Family, Religious Community, Church, Self, and Friends

"Alienation" is an overused word these days, but it is quite appropriate in the context of this discussion. Many activists find themselves withdrawing from those persons and institutions to which they formerly were strongly attached and with which they strongly identified. Alienation is experienced from family and friends, their church, their nation, and themselves. For women and men religious, there also can be alienation from their religious congregations as well. The aspects of this alienation include questionable authenticity, differences in lifestyle, lack of real or perceived support, and "we-they" perceptions.

There are dominant images for a health care worker, lawyer, member of a faith community, a church worker, or even a minister which are propounded by tradition, training, and popular opinion. Past and present institutional needs, professional behaviors, and apostolic commitments play a crucial part in defining these roles. In parishes, the professions, ministry training, or religious congregation a process of socialization occurs, of passing on a structured reality from one person or group to successors. We internalize certain images of what it means to be an active church member, a professional, or person in ministry: how one lives, relates to people, and works in society.[29]

The effect of this internalization is that those who break from these patterns may have to pay a very high price for their independence. Peer-acceptance is not as readily forthcoming for those who live differently, work in different settings, perform different ministries, or even dress differently. This is true for those who engage in any kind of nontraditional work that is unfamiliar to those in the mainstream of a community.

Many lay women and men in volunteer communities in poor neighborhoods or Catholic Worker houses may experience alienation from friends and family who are even afraid to visit their home or place of work. Often parents and friends express a mixture of feelings that run from concern for the activist's health or safety, to criticism of their financial responsibility, to powerful disagreement with their advocacy for social change. Married couples who choose to live among the poor and to raise their families in poorer neighborhoods or in racially or ethnically separated communities can experience the same gulf dividing them from friends and relatives whose experience is so different.

This problem of identity and authenticity is also experienced by social activists in religious congregations who do not share with their sisters or brothers the communality of engaging in a traditional religious work of their congregation, such as education or health care. Ironically, activists in religious congregations often self-affirm the alienation which they experience from their fellow religious. Since they, too, have internalized the common image of a professional religious, they experience strong visceral doubts about the authenticity and legitimacy of their own work. They doubt themselves as women or men religious. This reaction occurs despite the fact that extensive authority supports their social justice work—popes, councils, and sources within their own congregations.

Their alienation from religious companions may have another source hinted at earlier: lifestyle. On the one hand is the traditional institution-related community of religious sisters, brothers, or priests living a more middle-class, servant-ed existence on a campus or near a retreat house or health care facility. On the other hand there is a sim-

pler, self-serviced style of community located in a poor neighborhood
or rural community. Both lifestyles in a sense are structured by
the work or ministry itself. More critical, however, is the often distinct
feel to the different communities, including religious practices, mutuality of expectations and permissions, and service. These are what ultimately constitute at-home-ness. In former times religious moved about
from assignment to assignment with only limited readjustments in personal style; now, the move from traditional school community to inner-
city community or vice versa cannot be done now without significant
personal changes.

The feeling of alienation on the part of lay or religious social activists
can be reinforced by a perception of the absence of actual support from
others outside their work community. This perception has several causes separating those in work for social change and others: very few contacts with one another; little mutual interest in or understanding of
respective work or ministries; and physical isolation from one another's
places of work and residence. Those in other, more traditional, ministries in the church or a religious congregation may themselves feel
threatened by activists. They may even be hostile to their work. Or,
those others may simply be so caught up in the demands of their own
works that they cannot offer support, even if they knew how. One sister
in an inner-city community told me, for example, that despite the fact
that their community annually invited the many other members of their
religious congregation working in the same city to come to their house
for a party, very few had ever made the trip. Whatever the cause, it is
easy for the activist or activist community to begin to feel that friends,
family, or others in their church or community do not support them.

As activists become more and more conscious of, and sensitive to,
the structural and systemic features of the problems facing the poor,
they can move easily to a we-they conflict analysis of all American society—including the church, their own parish, or their religious congregation. William J. Byron, former president of Catholic University,
posed this consideration for members of his religious congregation
examining their works in the light of social inequities:

> Midway in this paper I asked, "Is our corporate apostolic service com-
> pensatory; are we throwing our weight onto the side of the oppressed?"
> Symbolically, justice is represented by trays in balance on a scale. The
> unbalance of social injustice, where one group's advantage (the down
> tray) is taken at the expense of another group (the up tray), calls for
> compensatory action....We see gaps between rich and poor, powerful
> and powerless, advantaged and disadvantaged. In exercising our min-

istry of justice, by whatever apostolic instruments, we should...[choose] to be—with Christ and as Christ—on the short side of all those gaps. Where do we throw our weight? Where do we throw our wealth, our income, our apostolic energy?[30]

Many activists answer Byron's question by saying that the churches and many religious congregations largely cast their weight with the "haves." They see the institutional, fiscal, and personnel weight of the churches and communities lined up with the advantaged in such practical and real dichotomies as these:

white v. black

white v. brown

male v. female

U. S. v. Third World

powerful v. powerless

rich v. poor

suburban v. urban

well-educated v. poorly educated

Activists conclude that no matter how much churches and communities tinker with their present institutional commitments to facilitate the entry of some minority composed of the poor or disadvantaged, institutional weight is still cast overwhelmingly on the side of the well-off.[31]

The alienation which activists experience also is rooted in the secular environment in which they often work and changes which occur in both religious identity and religious practices. More than their contemporaries in church parish or religious communities, many activists often move in an ecumenical and even secular world. The people they work for and with are often Protestants, Jews, agnostics, or atheists. The collaboration with these groups can contrast ironically with the experience of alienation from their own coreligionists. Even those deemed "enemies" such as some landlords, loan companies, corporations, banks, and city hall, often are strongly Catholic with significant ties to church, religious community, or institution.

Activists then can easily identify religiously with those whose lives mirror at least the social values of the gospel, namely the poor and those who take their stand with them. Here, among these groups at least, there seems to be no ambiguity for the believing activist. This deepens the experience of alienation from those others in their own

church whose religion the activist sees as privatized. This also subtly
affects the activist's own faith commitment, at least in some of its
more explicitly "religious" aspects.[32] As Gustavo Gutierrez notes:

> For many the participation in the process of liberation causes a weary-
> ing, anguished, long, and unbearable dichotomy between their life of
> faith and their revolutionary commitment....Moreover, the close collab-
> oration with people of different spiritual outlooks which this option
> provides leads one to ponder the contribution proper to the faith.[33]

This experience can shatter presuppositions about who are the saved,
who are really Christians, and what is ministry.

As activists apply a measuring-stick of the gospel of **faithjustice** to
those around them, the size of their church dwindles rapidly. This is
accompanied by the feeling of uneasiness and even anger with the
prayer and worship of the seemingly more inclusive brethren of their
church. As one author put it, "Submerged in the raw brutality of urban
poverty, the minister quickly develops a special bitterness toward that
decorative spirituality which hides indecision and evasion."[34] Small circles of fellow worshipers and prayer groups develop among those who
seem to be committed to the poor by their actual living. These may be
lay or religious or priests, or any combination. They may also be
Catholic, Protestant, Jewish, and non-formal believers. This development parallels the other kinds of narrowing of the world of the activist
indicated earlier.

An alternative reaction may be a skepticism toward, or even a total
rejection of, prayer and the spiritual life. Not only do these realities
become associated with evasion and other-worldliness, but they are
made all the more difficult by the **imperative** of the needs of the poor
and experiences of failure:

> But the continued wrestling with unyielding problems rips a man apart.
> It is true that such virile disregard of self counteracts the abstract dedi-
> cation of the church's official proclamation of "preferential love of the
> poor." For the individual minister, though, it brings its own brand of
> spiritual torture. Feelings of deadness—physical, psychological and spiri-
> tual—are inevitably born from failure and fatigue. When a brother's
> blood has spurted out and splashed you, however, one feels guilty in
> retreating from the combat—even for prayer.[35]

What can happen then is a move to a one-dimensional horizontal
Christianity whose demand is a total and complete dedication to "the

effective realization of this love in the city's barren world of shabbiness...."[36]

Both of the above two reactions have internal repercussions. They clash with the activist's prior and fundamental interior values of church universal and formal prayer, with images of ministry, religious life, or priestly service. This clash is the source of a deep-rooted discomfort and alienation within some activists. Their current experience does not jell with their past. If they are unable to come to a new synthesis that speaks to the internal pain, they again will incline to abandon present social ministry in an attempt to reclaim their past.

Alternatively, they may abandon their past in their church in an attempt to claim their present and future. This alienation from the church may be aggravated further by the actual opposition or interference of church leadership. This can take the form of attempting to prevent the work of the activist or to set requirements for that work more appropriate in other contexts.

Theoretical and Theological Underpinnings

In moving to the question of theory and theology, this chapter ventures even further from the descriptive to the analytical, and therefore to the more tentative. Nevertheless, the activist's underlying theoretical or theological beliefs have much to do with choice of ministry, evaluation of effectiveness, and eventual survival. In addition, a discussion of these matters necessarily addresses spirituality. This applies as well to formal non-believers. They usually have some deeply held values which effectively serve in place of theology and inform their spiritual life, namely their fundamental attitudes toward others, life, history, time, meaning, and self-value. In a very real sense, religious experience, spirituality, and theology are all correlates. Each affects the shape and substance of the others and in turn is shaped and given substance by them. Problems in one area invariably have an impact in the other two, usually creating parallel problems.

For the person of faith, three basic problem areas arise in working for social change that demand an adequate theory and theology: (1) power and conflict; (2) utopianism and ideology; and (3) dualism. Unless activists have some explicit or implicit framework for solving or at least living with these problems, they will experience serious unsettling when confronted by them. This unsettling further aggravates their dilemma.

One reaction repeated often by those in community organizing is that of being frightened of the use of power. They find it inconsistent with gospel values. They have "gentleness breakdowns." There is a similar reaction to the advocacy of conflict, as distinct from physical violence, which lies at the heart of not only community organizing, but also our adversary legal system, most urban politics, and much social theory, especially under Marxist and other influences. Some activists, both lay and clerical, find this advocacy inconsistent with their Christianity and their concept of ministry, reconciliation, and peacefulness. Nice people simply don't cause trouble!

Those of us who are engaged in working for social change must ask ourselves whether this apparently spontaneous reaction is true to the mark, articulating the truly Christian. We must examine the utilization of power in the context of conflict, asking whether it is congruent with the proclamation of the gospel of Jesus. One conclusion may be that the use of power and the engagement in conflict are both inappropriate, whether in certain concrete situations or always. This is akin to a pacifist stance that has strong roots in Christian history, and it is the response of some people to both power and conflict.

On the other hand, activists may conclude that this spontaneous aversion for power or conflict is simplistic and too idealistic. It indicates that the proponents of such a position have an inadequate social theology or ethics. They are reading the gospel too literally and lack a sufficiently comprehensive moral theology to meet the demands of real life. They fail to acknowledge the permanent presence of evil in the world and the need to confront it directly.

In concrete political history, then, they may conclude that pursuit of the good not only allows but requires the use of power or engagement in conflict. This is one way of understanding and following in the confrontational tradition of the prophets and of Jesus of Nazareth. If they do reach this last point, they will be faced with further questions of when and where and how much power or conflict are appropriate. In considering each and all of these questions, the activist's initial response of caution or even repugnance can act as a useful critical consciousness that tests and strains all attempts at formulating responses or answers. Whatever the conclusion, we activists must move beyond our initial and instinctive reaction against the use of power and the engagement in conflict. We must ask serious questions about the intersection of the gospel, ethics, and politics. If not, then we can be caught in a bind that will not allow us to continue our commitment to social justice ministry. We will burn out. (See more on power in Chapter Four.)

A second jarring clash experienced by some activists occurs between the theoretical utopianism of a new world or belief in the impending reign of God and the factual complexity, temporality, and failure involved in the processes of social change. A French worker-priest explains:

> I believe that the risk of the experience [of the clash of the ideal and the real in social change work] is greater for those who come from outside—motivated by idealism or ideology—and who mistake their desires for realities and their hopes for possibilities of immediate action. Men who are born in oppression and poverty and who have become aware of their plight are better armed to survive, despite the odds and against all opposition....I am distrustful of the enthusiasts and the programs of idealists of all sorts; or at least I fear for them and for the people who invest their lives in following them.[37]

If their pure utopianism cannot adequately incorporate the phenomenon of failure, these activists are in jeopardy. If their theological stance cannot encompass the advocacy of solutions both complex and provisional, which are often the only solutions that work, their commitment is at risk.

How can those working for social change make a judgment to begin one specific course of action or to continue another if their only concrete choices are unacceptable within a pure ideological or theological framework? The inability to reconcile or to live with this tension between the ideal and the real was an important factor in the experience of many ex-activists. They embraced their work with grand hopes and enthusiasm and abandoned it, sometimes after only a brief stint, disillusioned and bitter.

Eventually, to survive, those committed to social justice must ask themselves how the tentative solution and the failed endeavor fit into their social theory and theology. They have to deal with the frustration and paralysis created by their own absolutes, and apply to their own rigid ideological structures the same liberating standards of criticism they might use on some other oppressive social structure. This very endeavor is a walking beneath the cross. For many activists, such self-criticism will be very painful. The liberation of grace, however, always encompasses an element of pain when it moves us away from ready answers to which we are securely anchored and forces us into the unknown where we must steer without certainty. This pain and uncertainty, however, can connect us more closely to those whose daily lives are weighed down in poverty and whose options are almost always limited by a lack of resources.

The final critical theological challenge is dualism. Here the activist formally confronts a subtle problem which seems to lie at the heart of various specific difficulties discussed earlier. In the arena of prayer, for example, the tension can arise between so-called vertical and horizontal Christianity, our relation to God over against our relation to others. For example, the pressing needs of persons in pain can make prayer seem to be so much idle neglect and escapism. Really committed people simply do not have the time or the leisure for prayer! Authenticity is a second area of dualism, and the separation is experienced between church, on the one hand, and involvement in the secular world on the other. In a third context of religious identity, the dualism arises between many religious practices and the social activist's immersion in the work and life of the poor.

This same dualism, posed alternately as church/world or sacred/profane, is central to the feeling of some priests, brothers, or sisters in social action work that it is somehow only **natural**. Against this assessment, they may feel called by their baptisms, ordinations, or vows to mediate the supernatural in more traditional sacramental ministry and overt preaching. Even if they have become accustomed to the tension or have resolved it personally, friends and foes resurface it by asking, "How is what you do priestly (or religious, or ministerial)?" Ironically, laypeople in parish social ministry get asked the inverse, "Don't only priests and nuns work in parishes?"

In one sense, this is the classic incarnational question and it situates the activist firmly in the midst of Christian tradition. Belief in the incarnation of God in Christ Jesus, and in the ongoing presence and action of God in the Spirit, grounds an attitude that resists separating the human from the divine. Christian spirituality, at its best, sees divine and human action blended in a single vision and movement across history. There are then no merely natural endeavors which are divorced from the presence and action of divine grace. More specifically, the Judaeo-Christian tradition, in teaching **faithjustice**, explicitly ties the reign of God to action for justice and peace in society.

The fact that the question about the divine and the human has been asked before, even for centuries, does not make the answer any easier. This very persistence testifies to the difficulty of bridging this sacred/profane dualism. The inability or failure to respond can be costly for activists. They must be prepared to deal with this question, whether posed by others or in their own experience. In responding, they may choose to formulate answers, or to argue that the questions themselves are misleading and arise out of false, dualistic presuppositions. This requires serious prayerful study and reflection. It means grappling with such concepts as the universality of grace, the implications of the incarnation for human living, and the human role in the plan of salvation.

These three theological/theoretical questions, dealing with power and conflict, utopianism and pragmatism, and dualism, are connected. All demand a complex response which is neither easily formulated nor readily at hand. Moreover, that response must be both practical and organic for each person. It must become so integrated into that person's own spirituality that it can weather the cycle of poverty, the animosity of comfortable coreligionists, and the ups and downs of working for social change.

Successful activists seem to have built their spirituality upon at least an implicit resolution of these problems. They could help themselves and others immensely if they would articulate their experience and spell out their integrated vision. Some others, on the contrary, are still caught up in the questioning. This uncertainty, coupled with alienating experiences and the strains associated with work for social change, constitutes the critical burnout dilemma. If activists cannot fashion an adequate support system, or cope with those forces threatening alienation, or address the questions of theology and spirituality, they cannot survive at what they do. They will not be able to carry on the work of social action effectively, not as whole persons, and certainly not for long.

Organizational and Environmental Factors in Burnout

While some studies of burnout causality have been made, they have tended to be dominated by a psychological perspective which focused on the individuals affected[38] or on interpersonal factors such as role clarifications. In so doing, "the emphasis continues to be on blaming the victim" by implying "that both problem and solution reside in the person."[39] Solutions or preventive measures continue to be person-focused. They center on such efforts as stress management exercises, support groups, and screening and training of staff who will be in frequent contact with clients. Newer research and analysis, however, suggest that the focus on burnout must shift from individual activists and personal causes and cures to the organizations in which they work.[40]

That seems to be an important corrective and to reflect the social analysis called for by the Pastoral Circle.

These newer insights would shift our attention to organizational and environmental influences upon burnout under at least three headings: shared responsibility, role and organizational conflict, and inadequate professional development. In recent studies of a congregation of women religious and of helping persons in the field of aging, the most significant organizational characteristic atop the list of factors associated with burnout was shared responsibility.[41] Inversely, that is. The higher the level of shared responsibility, the lower the burnout experienced among those in the working group. This finding underscores the importance of structuring collaborative processes into the operation of various social service and advocacy projects, from the parish emergency assistance network to the local legal services program.

This finding is highly congruent with the tradition of Catholic social teaching, with that tradition's stress upon both human dignity and freedom and upon the principle of subsidiarity. This principle stresses the importance of making decisions at the lowest effective level. This finding also resonates with recent studies on the morale of the Catholic clergy in the U.S., including the most recent study by the National Conference of Catholic Bishops. The bishops' study listed its first area of response to morale problems under the heading of "Ownership and Participation."[42]

The second most important environmental factor correlating with burnout seems to be the existence of role and organizational conflict. In this regard, those persons with positive styles of coping with conflict seemed to mitigate burnout most effectively. Those coping skills would include dealing directly with issues, negotiating differences, and seeking consultation. Persons with passive or defensive styles such as redefining their own role without communicating with others, disengaging, and avoidance, were likely to score high on the burnout indicators.[43]

One particular application of this finding touches upon what is called **emergent role theory**. This theory associates conflict with newly developing positions and the lack of clarity and conflicting expectations which frequently accompany them in the workplace.[44] While this is certainly applicable to newly emerging roles in the church, it is true as well of new advocacy groups, volunteers in church and secular agencies, and new professions arising in response to problems of poverty in our society (e.g., community organizers). Conflicting and changing role expectations was the number one problem listed in the recent report on clergy morale. The clergy reported on themselves in terms of, "many feeling trapped, overworked, frustrated and with the sense of little or no time for themselves."[45]

Recent studies also indicate a high correlation between the absence of staff development and burnout. This finding would recommend, first, strong initial preparation for careers in the helping professions and in social change advocacy. It also commends continuing professional development while on the job and specialized training in preparation for career changes, sometimes called, "retooling."[46] Too many religious communities, for instance, take schoolteachers or pastors from white, middle-class institutions and communities and thrust them, completely unprepared except by generous willingness, into inner-city ghettoes or third world communities. The results are too often horrendous for both the missioning and the receiving communities. Programs and norms need to be developed for initial and continuing education of staff and volunteers in a wide range of activities within social justice work. It would mean introducing some elements of a professionalism for the long haul.[47]

Problems of professional development, role conflict, and shared responsibility are all made more difficult in, and by the very nature of, many organizations and agencies working for social change. Such organizations, a great number of which have only short histories, are often underfunded and overwhelmed by client demands and high staff turnover. They frequently have not had time for the development of middle managers. They are often administered by upper and middle level managers who recently were caseworkers, staff attorneys, and other service providers. Good at client service and advocacy, these women and men often are promoted to management without requisite skills or experience. And management training is often a low budget priority. This management weakness, combined with other resource deprivation, can mean that other serious structural problems are not addressed, to the detriment of both managers and staff.

Signs of Hopefulness

This often negative discussion has been designed specifically to sketch out the elements of what is a contemporary dilemma, even a crisis. It is as well an attempt to initiate a process of dialogue and discussion among those in social ministry that will facilitate healthy responses. They will be helped if its challenge is picked up by the more experienced and the more expert: the psychologists, spiritual directors, theologians, social scientists, and, most importantly, veteran activists themselves. Hopeful responses surely have been developing among those who have recognized the seriousness of the problem of burnout. A brief sampling of these developments follows:

1. People are discussing this dilemma. Many are alert to the problems, raising questions and positing solutions in professional journals and association meetings.[48] In a sense, this is the most helpful of the signs since it suggests that activists will not be mere passive and unknowing victims of these destructive forces in their lives.

2. Serious theologians are addressing these problems. The first sentences of the Introduction to Gutierrez's **A Theology of Liberation**, written twenty years ago, is:

> This book is an attempt at reflection, based on the Gospel and the experiences of men and women committed to the process of liberation in the oppressed and exploited land of Latin America. It is the theological reflection born of shared efforts to abolish the current unjust situation and to build a different society, freer and more human.[49]

The works of Gutierrez and others seriously address many of the problems indicated above, especially those in the theoretical and theological area. These offer genuine hope, especially when coupled with the renewed interest among activists in developing a theology and spirituality which will support their own work. This marriage of theology and practice itself may be a good example of just what the blending and interplay of theory and praxis are all about.

3. Activists recently have displayed a much more intense interest in community life (a subject for later chapters), a development supported by recent research on burnout.[50] This experience among both lay and religious women and men harbors real promise. It should foster current apostolic effectiveness, and also promote the personal stability which will support more innovative endeavors in terms of work, lifestyle, and spirituality. At the very least, this development provides an important locus for expressing and sharing feelings of anger and frustration. Studies have indicated that burnout rates are lower for those who are able to express, analyze, and share their feelings about work with their colleagues. Finally, communities can counter experiences of alienation and non-support.

4. Developments in community building have been accompanied by an intense interest on the part of some religious congregations in putting together apostolic team efforts in response to social problems. This lays the groundwork for more longevity of various social projects.

It helps to move past the maverick status of some past social justice efforts and carries them to a new stage more proper to modeling for, and training of, new generations of religious and lay social activists.

5. Ministry training programs in dioceses and in religious congregations are providing to younger persons a variety of diverse cultural experiences, especially by working and/or living among the poor. When this is supplemented with reflection upon social realities and the acquisition of genuine helping-skills, these people should be prepared better for encountering the harsh realities of American poverty and injustice.

This development also suggests a brief remark on the element of competence in social ministry. In missioning persons to, or choosing, social ministry, serious consideration must be given to professional and personal competence. Professional capability means the acquisition of skills and knowledge helpful to the work in question. Personal competence, however, refers to individual growth and character development such as to improve the fit between a person and a specific work for social justice. Attention to competence, of course, will not eliminate entirely the experiences of failure or frustration or other stresses. But careful selection and preparation, combined with support systems, can help them to survive and even prosper in this work.

6. The growing and liberating realization of the limits and appropriateness of the conflict model in social ministry is also a positive indicator. Activists have found that they cannot remain true to their own experience of life and people if they absolutize the evil of the oppressors or the goodness of the oppressed. Simultaneously, however, they are accepting the existence of evil and structures of evil that must be anticipated, recognized, and confronted directly in pastoral planning and action.

7. More difficult to capture here is a growing realization of the persistence of failure in all social-change ministry. More and more activists realize that experiences of failure must be integrated positively into their spirituality without having such an awareness become an excuse for social irresponsibility and inaction. Efforts in this direction include reflective evaluation of redemptive suffering in Christian theology, a dynamic theology of development and history, as well as an understanding of the incarnation that truly melds the creative activity of humanity with the grace of God active in history. The consideration of failure, however, is only one example of the increasing awareness of the need for every activist to develop both a social anthropology and a theology adequate for this work.

8. Another development on the contemporary scene that offers hope is the growing awareness of many people of their serious obligation to respond actively to the problems of the poor and to oppressive social structures. There also is a keen interest in simplicity of lifestyle and "small is beautiful" among some people. These developments may help ease the tensions experienced between lay social justice communities and families and their friends and relatives. In some religious congregations, there have been new moves to a poorer, self-servicing lifestyle in religious formation and other communities. This modest change alone may well ease the alienation described above in terms of different styles of at-home-ness between activists and the other members of their religious congregation. The very fact that a number of religious denominations issued statements on economic and social justice in the past ten years also provides a common background for faith-dialogue between activists and others in U.S. faith communities.

9. A refreshing interest in prayer and reflection exists among many social activists. Attempts have been made to develop genuine expressions of spirituality which directly support their lives among the poor. These newer forms are attuned to the universality of the Christian mystery, as well as to the preferential option for the poor, the centrality of the reign of God, and the ambiguity of total involvement in the **now** and of eschatological hope in the **not yet**. For some, this is helped by constantly situating parish and community liturgy and their own personal prayer in the current social context. For others, renewed prayer means experimenting with retreats specifically attending to the social reality, or fasting and abstaining attuned to world hunger and food costs, or prayer and liturgies in the African American or Hispanic American genre, or scripture services prompted by local, national, and world political events. Still others have found nurturance in Native American spirituality that reverences the gifts of the natural earth and underscores communal environmental responsibility as well. A growing seriousness about interiority is necessary to fashion a viable and vibrant spirituality for a new and unknown future.[51]

10. The attention of recent research to organizational and environmental influences on burnout underscores the efforts of a number of social activists to scrutinize more closely the organizations and agencies to which they belong. These efforts include attention to role clarifications, better sharing of responsibilities, adequate training for management and all staff, review of salaries and benefits, sabbatical policies personnel policies in keeping with the mission of the organization, and development of support systems for staff.

11. Much thought and reflection in books and articles has gone into developing a social spirituality over these last ten or fifteen years. Many official church authorities as well have gone on record recently with a theology of social and economic justice. These pronouncements not only help the activists to formulate their own personal framework, but they also validate specific work for social justice and the broader commitment of the churches to **faithjustice**. That cannot but give support to individual activists.

Conclusion

It seems unnecessary at this point to go further into the burnout phenomenon. There are ample articles, workshops, and other resources available. What is fascinating about the more recent research on organizational and environmental factors is its consonance with the insight developed in both recent secular writings and church documents about the intricate and powerful connection between persons and structures. In this case the tie is between the person who chooses to stand with the poor and the very organization or agency within which she or he is working. This discussion also introduces us into the topics of chapter two, where we will look more closely at the nature of social and cultural institutions and structures, and chapter three, where we will see, not the dyad of person and institution, but a triadic connection between persons, small groups and structures, and larger social-structural systems.

Veteran social activist and sojourner Joyce Hollyday offers us a final hopeful thought about our response to the risk of burnout:

> And I thought, "It all comes down to this—
> lighting candles for one another
> keeping each other burning bright,
> rather than letting each other burn out."
> It's a task related to joy—
> to creating space for celebration
> helping each other to laugh
> when things don't turn out quite right,
> and living with a sense of awe and gratitude
> for God's goodness.[52]

CHAPTER TWO

Making Connections

As for what we can accomplish, our capacity for societal guidance
depends on how much of ourselves we are willing to invest in understanding the societal system and its guidance mechanisms and to what
extent we can organize ourselves to act on this understanding.

AMITAI ETZIONI
SOCIAL PROBLEMS[1]

*When Dr. Martin Luther King, Jr., began to speak out against the war in
Vietnam just before his death, I was deeply disappointed. As a young south-
erner with a keen interest in his role in the struggle for racial justice, I felt
that this move into foreign affairs would confuse his clear stand on race,
muddy the waters, and undermine his national leadership. Then, too, my
father had been in the navy during World War II; and my older brother
fought in the navy off Vietnam in the late sixties. Those family commitments
and the typical southern romanticism about things military (I had imagined
myself going to the Naval Academy at Annapolis as a young boy) also slowed
my own recognition of the intimate connections between domestic social concerns and military and foreign policy.*

* * *

*In 1977, I was visiting California and had the opportunity to see the
giant sequoias in one national forest. While we were there, a ranger told us a
story about their care of the trees. To preserve these giant trees, the forest service had carefully protected them from fires caused by lightning, human care-
lessness, or other causes. Some of the greatest of the trees in fact were scarred
from old fires. This prevention program was designed to end scarring and
even more tragic total tree loss.*

*After an extended period, forest specialists noticed that there were no baby
trees. After much consideration, it became clear that the only significant
change in the environment was the campaign to prevent fires. Further investi-*

gation revealed that, besides the scarring of the trees, most fires did not effect serious tree damage. Started mostly by lightning, the fires actually cleared the forest floor of the natural debris from fallen needles, leaves, bark, and branches. This accumulation, called "duff," turned out to be the miscreant. What the tree protectors did not realize was that the seeds of the trees, when they fell, put out about a 12 inch root. The duff piled on the forest floor, however, due to the fire fighting program, had accumulated to a depth exceeding twelve inches. When the fallen seed extended its root, it wasn't touching fertile ground because of this thick covering. Thus, no baby trees.

Taking a lesson from nature, the rangers are now setting controlled fires in these forests. They are burning off the duff, just as nature had done. The result? Baby trees!

* * *

One of the harder lessons of my days stalking the halls of the Georgia legislature was that, on all but a few classically interracial issues like minority contracts and Aid to Families with Dependent Children, black and poor issues were not the same. True, a disproportionate percentage of the black community was poor. True, the average incomes of black and white communities were and remain very unequal. Nevertheless, when it came to landlord-tenant issues, I found that some black legislators, themselves landlords, could be as insensitive to poor tenants as white ones. Some black nursing home owners were as resistant to nursing home residents' rights as others. Some black lenders or insurers were hard as nails on consumers' rights, and so forth. I began to realize that wealth could erect and enforce segregation and injustice as rigidly as race had ever done.

* * *

One of the Cinderella dreams of certain classes of young women in New Orleans is to be selected queen of a Mardi Gras ball, a chance for a day of celebration and honor–even if make-believe. In 1987, one so honored was a senior whom I knew at a small Catholic prep school. At the somewhat tardy invitation of the Mardi Gras organization, this young queen-to-be submitted her list of guests for the ball, including all of her classmates. After all, she told me, their years as classmates would soon be over. They could share this celebration as one fond memory of growing up and becoming young adults together.

The embarrassed caller to the queen's mother informed her that NOT ALL of her daughter's guests could be included, since they were not all white. Would the queen mind striking the offending guest from her invitation list?[2] The queen-to-be would not...and thus goes the tale.

Family members were embarrassed. The board of the organization–including *prominent Catholics and relatives of the queen–refused **even one invitation** to a young black girl to sit with her classmates to watch the evening's festivities. School classmates who were maids in the queen's court were reluctant to join her plea for a policy change. The queen-to-be thus relinquished her Cinderella dream two weeks before the ball.*

This unpublicized event was not a great social protest, nor a young radical's attempt to make a statement about the pervasive structures of racism in our society. She had lived with it all around her for much of her young life. Like Rosa Parks, though, who sat down in forbidden vacant seats on a Montgomery bus just because her feet hurt, this was one more individual saying, "It's just not right." As the would-be queen told me, "I was supposed to make a presentation on South African apartheid for class that week. It just seemed hypocritical."

The Social Analysis Moment: What It Is

Perhaps the key moment on the Pastoral Circle is social analysis. Social analysis is one-half of the answer to the question, "What is really going on in this situation?" Beyond mere description, this point in the process focuses on trying to understand and analyze a situation, problem, or dilemma more carefully. Holland and Henriot define social analysis as "the effort to obtain a more complete picture of a social situation by exploring its **historical and structural relationships**."[3]

This could seem to be a complex task. Brazilian Francisco Ivern says social analysis requires use of philosophy and the social sciences, including not only economics, sociology, and political science, but also social psychology, religious sociology, and cultural anthropology.[4] One Vatican source speaks of a "plurality of methods and viewpoints, each of which reveals only one aspect of reality which is so complex that it defies simple and univocal explanation."[5] The Holland-Henriot approach to social analysis seems to me to be shorthand for socioeconomic-political-cultural-religious-historical analysis.

Such a broad understanding suggests the need for experts to do analysis. It also implies transcending any particular expertise in ways that return social analysis to the hands of each of us as concerned citizens. Thomas Clarke concurs:

> Social analysis is not the prerogative of an elite. If a participatory, democratic way of life is to be a possibility, it requires a basic confidence and skill on the part of ordinary people in making critical and informed judgments regarding the social contexts of their lives. To say this is not

to deny the importance of specialized knowledge, or the difficulty which most of us have in being reasonably well informed on scores of major and complex issues, and in deciding just what sources of information and analytical helps to critical judgment deserve our trust.[6]

Clarke argues that specialists in the various disciplines are "helpful mentors," but not substitutes for our own judgments. These judgments have to be built upon experience and combined with values and commitments which are unique to each one of us.

Social analysis, however, helps us "move beyond personal experience of the milieu and to provide us with the empirical and analytical basis for the evaluative judgments and the pragmatic decisions which will represent our response of faith to the needs of our times."[7] Without such analysis, Clarke adds, we risk "visionary, romantic or simply misguided and irrelevant" decisions. With such analysis, Joseph Daoust adds, we can "gradually remove the limitations of our cultural blinders, and make us more critically aware of the social structures which must be transformed to 'make clear the way of the Lord.'"[8]

I like to think of social analysis as asking the journalist's questions: who, what, why, when, where, and how? The first paragraph of a standard press story often answers all these questions. The point of social analysis is to ask those same questions about whatever we are involved in. This applies to what is in the local news, and to national and international public policy. Social analysis, while the technical phrase may initially put us off, is just that—asking the right questions.

The next and related moment of theological reflection will build upon analysis and ask, what are the values here? How do I and my faith community judge what's graced or sinful? What is freeing or enslaving people? What promotes or destroys human dignity and covenant community? Before entering into theological reflection, however, our task is to apply our senses, understood broadly, to the reality around us. It is scientific inquiry; it is doctors diagnosing patients; it is a child asking, "Why, Mommie?"

When many people hear about social analysis they protest, "Oh, I can't do that; it takes an economist or a political scientist; I don't have the skills." The reality is that we are all doing social analysis in a wide variety of situations. We promote explicit social analysis here to call attention to the fact that we do analysis now and thus to improve what we do in the future. This chapter also introduces a relatively simple way to enter into this effort, using journalism's basic questions.

The Evangelical Importance of Social Analysis

We do social analysis to better understand our part in bringing forth the reign of God in history, to better know what is graced or sinful. Peter Marchetti uses the traditional Ignatian spiritual term **discreta caritas** for this endeavor: discerning love.[9] To engage in the art and science of social analysis is to try to love wisely, an exercise in natural and supernatural prudence. This is not just love, but discerning love. It is not just enough to say we love, to feel love, or even to give my body over to martyrdom. This is especially true when we dare to say, "I love the poor," for whom misguided love is too often like one more instance of deficient housing, second-class medical care, hand-me-down clothing, or shoddy merchandise.

Social analysis says my love is serious enough to want to discern, "What is really helpful in this situation?" Social analysis is an instrument for standing with the poor which sharpens the vision that enables us to see differently and clears our thinking to judge differently what we see. Too many well-intentioned people have begun volunteer work among the poor or accepted positions in poor parishes or poor schools without an understanding "what is really happening here." When they fail to do so, they often find themselves part of the problem of alienation or paternalism, instead of being part of the solution. Social analysis is an important necessary step in shaping a response that asks, what is discerning and effective love for me?

If we look again at the Pastoral Circle, my sequoias story can give us a better feel for the task of analysis. We begin with a human experience of fires and scarred or even destroyed trees. The perception is that fires are a major threat to a valued creation. The analysis, reflection, and decision-making is simply that we have the capacity for controlling fires, that maintaining the trees is an important value for us, and so we decide to prevent forest fires. Simple.

Then, however, we take another turn around the circle. The experience of fire-fighting, caring more intensely for these great trees, gives rise to a new experience: the absence of seedling trees. This constitutes new datum for analysis. With this, the previous decision to act is reassessed. Then there is a move from understanding the seeding process and the impact of the duff to the role that fires had played in eliminating the duff. And a new decision arises: to set fires, imitating nature.

It is important to note here that the same set of values are operative in both situations as we move around the Pastoral Circle. We value our environment; we treasure the beauty of the giant trees; we want to preserve them for posterity. What changed was the analysis of what in reality would enhance the values we professed. **Desire and effort alone are not enough.**

Now the trees seem a safe example. How much unreflective, uncritical effort expended to promote the reign of God, or justice and peace, has actually resulted in the exact opposite! How often have well-intentioned efforts communicated destruction of human environments: of cultures, communities, and families. How unwittingly have our painfully destructive efforts painted for others a God who was hateful. One need only reflect on numerous instances when missionaries confused Christian faith with European culture and philosophical formulations.

The examples are legion. That is why we do social analysis, to somehow communicate what we really set out to do in the first place. It is an effort to evangelize effectively, to build and not tear down the reign of God, to re-create and not destroy the original blessing of Genesis.

Social analysis helps the church to do its job better, which is the preaching of the gospel. It encourages church people to distinguish the inculturation of the gospel from its acculturation. When inculturated, the gospel borrows the elements of human culture, permeates them, and proclaims a reign of God to be lived by human persons "profoundly linked to a culture."[10] When acculturated, the gospel becomes subject to cultural forces, pegged to fit cultural holes such as nationalistic and individualistic self-interest. For example, Americans are said now to be choosing religions as consumers. Their choices are distorted by cultural forces into either an individualistic retreat focusing on the inner person or a fundamentalistic adherence to an external salvation outside of self and the real world.[11] Both are powerfully shaped by individualism, and both retire the believer from social reality where the God Yahweh and the Lord Jesus summon us to action.

Social analysis enables those who exercise individual ministries such as counseling, spiritual direction, and even governance in the churches and religious congregations, to avoid being merely "good agents of socialization."[12] In that role in the past, their advice and direction often had been toward compliance, accommodation to the institution or system, and being a team player. If things were not working out, then obviously there was some personal trait or behavior which was the cause. Both cause and response were constrained within the personal sphere. As with the more recent research on burnout, social analysis can help those in ministry to see powerful social and institutional forces. The discernment of goodness, growth, and light then may well lead to advice focused on institutions and structures, rather than on individual behavior.

Holland and Henriot stress that, in the face of American pragmatism and its focus on the concrete here-and-now, social analysis can help promote true human solidarity.[13] Taking a longer, deeper view of reality, such analysis will tend to eschew fragmented piecemeal gains for an individual or a local group in the interest of "permanent, long-range, holistic gains by all."[14] It will also help us to see the connections between issues, as when Dr. Martin Luther King spoke out against the Vietnam War.

Social analysis also gives us a concrete handle for exercising the **hermeneutic of the *anawim***[15] that comes of standing with the poor. Instead of just a negative reaction toward the status quo or those in power positions, analysis provides us with instruments for understanding and assessment. Community organizer Saul Alinsky put it this way:

> I believe irreverence should be part of the democratic faith because in a free society everyone should be questioning and challenging. If I had to put up a religious symbol the way some people have crucifixes, or stars of David, my symbol would be the question mark. A question mark is a plowshare turned upside down. It plows your mind so that thoughts and ideas grow.[16]

Social analysis is one way we express Alinsky's question mark. It asks, "What's really going on here?" from various vantage points.

Ultimately, social analysis is about linkages, about making connections. Through analysis, we better understand the web of relationships that hold the human community and its sub-parts together. We see the connections between the U.S. and world communities, between economics and politics, between social, cultural, and religious forces, between "us" and various forms of "them," and between the life of faith and the pursuit of justice.

The "How To" of Social Analysis

The initial "how to" of social analysis is simple fact-finding, gathering as much information as we reasonably can. In many cases, the accumulated data will solve the question of what needs to be done in a situation. Many religious people want to make it much more difficult. They think proper decision-making requires going into the closet to wait for that whispered direction from the Lord. To others, social analysis means entering into some ponderous process of individual or communal discernment. Historically, discernment was a careful religious model for choosing between courses of action that could not be reasonably distinguished based upon the information available. Where the information available was decisive, discernment was to be avoided precisely because of its duration and complexity.

Often, people can decide logically between two courses of action when sufficient information has been gathered. The sequoias in California are a good example. Once those responsible realized that what they were doing was injuring the giant trees, it became obvious that they should choose another course of action. What distinguished their first course of action from the second was not better reflection or prayer, or a change in the values, but more complete information.

Lesson one, then, is to gather all the available facts. Often what we need to do may then become obvious. Collect as much information as is reasonably possible. Reasonably. The "paralysis of analysis," as it is called, can come from the inexhaustible nature of information and opinion that can be collected in the human sciences. A more helpful way to think of analysis, at least until some proficiency is gained, may be the "who, what, why, when, where, and how" of journalists.[17]

WHO AND WHAT

Our first questions—WHO and WHAT—basically ask what are the facets of the situation before us. This can be applied to a school, health clinic, neighborhood, community group, or political body. Who are the people involved? What are their characteristics: age, gender, ethnic group, race, occupation, and economic status? What do they do? What are the non-human entities: the organizations, budgets, formal and informal rules, and ways of proceeding? How much money is involved, and whose is it? What facilities are involved, and who controls access?

At this stage, especially, it is important to ask a lot of questions and be persistent about it. This is especially true, often, when the person concerned about social reality is thrust into a new world of sorts. This is doubly important in entering the world of the poor. One key set of questions in that new environment is suggested by Holland and Henriot:

1. **Who makes the decisions?**
2. **Who benefits from the decisions?**
3. **Who bears the cost of the decisions?**[18]

The answers may be surprising. They often reveal the economic and political decision-making power that delineates real social classes even within our complex "classless" society. Answers to these three questions also will not be apparent in many situations, not without proceeding with further analysis. That process takes its initial energy from asking questions. As Saul Alinsky advised community organizers, "Actually you do more organizing with your ears than with your tongue."[19]

When I used to train younger legal services attorneys, I would tell them, "The way we all learned is asking questions." And I would relate a personal story. After a week of orientation, we new attorneys had been baptized in the cauldron of interviewing ten new clients a week. Sitting there at my desk under my brand new framed sheepskin, I had my legal pad ready. In comes my first client, ready to tell her story. I did all the introductory matters about confidentiality, checking information prepared for me by the receptionist, making sure it was correct.

Then came the fateful moment, "Well, now, what seems to be your problem?"

"Well, I'm having problems with my railroad retirement benefits." I said to myself, I don't have a clue about what railroad retirement benefits are. Now that I am Mr. Attorney, however, I'm not going to tell this client.

"Yes, I see," I responded knowingly. "Well, well, what railroad did you work for and when was that?" Looking as professional as possible, I asked my first set of logical questions, the good old familiar who, what, when, etc. Then, having satisfied myself that I did not know what to ask further, I excused myself to "check something in the library."

That trip to the library was really a panic run down the hall to the nearest lawyer in the office to ask, "WHAT ARE RAILROAD RETIRE-MENT BENEFITS?" When she explained that they were part of a program very similar to Social Security in structure and benefits, hearing and appeal rights, I began to know what to ask next, first of the more senior lawyer and then of the client. Asking questions was the trick. In my experience, I soon learned it was the only real way to get started, even before the essential trip to the law library to do research. Asking questions was the real school after the formality of law school.

This experience for new lawyers is similar to that of many people first working in the area of social injustice. The first stage is the same, and the key into the door of knowledge is asking questions, especially in any new environment. If something does not make sense about the way people are behaving, ask about it. You may not want to ask them directly. It may seem offensive. If so, ask an experienced co-worker, especially one from the local community. Ask one of the elders. Ask questions.

It's not just the who and what questions that need asking. People are far more complex than the stuff of mathematics:

> **Unlike** torpedoes and other technical systems, those elements subject to review and signaling in a society are not dead matter but individuals and groups of persons. For both normative **and** practical reasons, their feelings, preferences, values, and interests must be introduced **systematically** into the analysis.[20]

We need to find out about the issues at odds, the things of concern to people. What are the rules and policies around here, formal and informal? What pressures operate in the agency or church we may work in, and in the neighborhood? And we must ask about the key individuals, the important opinion and decision-makers, since they often are not the elected or formal leaders.

WHEN

Another framework for understanding what is going on and what might be done is history or time. The WHEN question. Asking when may not seem so important, but when-questions lay bare a lot of actual WHY and HOW in any situation. In the process, too, there is often revealed the present and the future and at least three senses of history and time.

Remembering the Past. One sense of our past answers the question, "What actually happened?" We might call this the first form of history. How did this railroad track come to run right through the middle of our neighborhood? What were the reasons for the strike? When was this organization begun? It's the quest for black history, or Native Americans trying to recapture their own tribal history. What actually happened? Surprisingly, this is often the hardest history to come to know, especially because of the other two histories operating in most groups.

The second and perhaps most significant history is what people remember. What is remembered is not necessarily what actually happened. People do not really remember for a number of reasons. We remember history selectively, as so many husbands and wives can assure us from their squabbles. But what we remember is often so much more important than what actually happened. This awareness is critically important in situations of injustice. The community worker must understand not only when and why the school board closed the neighborhood school, but also what people remember about it.

The third form of history is related to the second; it is a form of what we remember, but more formally shaped by what are called theories of history. There are straight line historical development theories, and history-is-cyclical theories, and Teilhardian theories of convergence, and God-has-it-all-in-hand theories. Salvation history, the narrative of God's relation to humanity in the Judaeo-Christian tradition, is one such formal historical theory. Central to historical theories are theories of change—three of which are discussed by Holland and Henriot under the headings of traditional, liberal, and radical.[21]

When asked how we assess change, we may perceive it to have been violent or peaceful, abrupt or gradual. How we judge past changes to have occurred will likely shape our own theory of what form change must take in the future to be effective. That future sense, however, may come from our studies of history or our experience of change in our own nation, community, or personal life. It may also turn on whether our present is secure or not:

> The past/future selection of viewpoint, in practice, seems most often to be dependent on the experience that an individual or community has had of life and society. To experience security and adequate provision and acceptance in the society normally means that one sees the societal structures as stable, the outcome of a satisfactory development. To experience exclusion, contempt, insecurity and inadequate provision, on the other hand, normally means that one has to interpret reality with reference to a better future as the object of hope and effort, and therefore that one has to see the present societal structure as instable because only in process of development.[22]

In addition, even our own disposition shapes our perception of past and future change. Some people are by temperament far more at home with change, and even animated by it. Their theories of history—and their futurizing—will be more inclined to be change-oriented, or at least comfortable with change.

Influencing our feel for history as well, is how we assess the dominant forces moving us all along or holding us back. The first of these is our perception or belief about the nature of the human person: good or evil; molding or molded by society's institutions; free or determined.[23] Critical institutions shape this sense of history. People may say, "Well, what has determined everything in this neighborhood has been the river." Or it has been the mill; or racial animosity; or the economy. Jobs have been generated or not, moved to the sun belt or across the ocean. The point is that much of our sense of history is shaped by theorizing of scholars or the crowd at the corner bar.

One useful method for individuals or groups to understand the past, despite even conflicting perceptions of others, is suggested by St. Ignatius of Loyola in his *Spiritual Exercises.* Our understanding of events can be deepened by asking three questions: (1) How did this start? (2) How did it end? and (3) What was our experience in the middle?[24] It seems simple enough. The point is that I can enhance my learning from the past by careful consideration of, not just the events that occurred, but my own and others' experiences in going through these events. This examination looks deeper into the thoughts, feelings, and beliefs of the actors involved at all stages of the proceedings.

This kind of analysis can forestall repeating the aggravating events, or be an early warning of conflicts in which we might intervene. Sometimes we can find out, watching chains of events, how to control the damage. Finally, successful or unsuccessful resolutions of problems can teach us about future peacemaking. By focusing on events in my own life, I can often learn more about communities in conflict or at peace, and community negotiations. In effect, I can learn to accomplish win/win outcomes that are models for larger peacemaking.

Intuiting the Future. The future is also part of this when-question, at least in the intuitive sense that people have about where we are going, individually and as a society. We first need to ask ourselves about the people we work with and how their sense of the future shapes their present. For juveniles on drugs, battered wives, and people living on the streets, how do they conceive of their future lives? What do they see happening in the larger society to affect them? What options do they have? What resources are within themselves to seize those options?

Answers to those questions are so often rooted deeply in past history. This is another reason that the concerned activist must share those stories to understand future possibilities. The perceived past is the mother of present possibilities and so often shapes our perception of the future. Inability to deal with past failures may make one person gun-shy about unknown futures. The young person who is the first member of her family to graduate from school may be willing to try new challenges. A community with past successes at organizing itself may consider a widespread rent strike or a militant anti-drug campaign.

The experience of the present also determines future possibilities as well. Numerous small children may keep a young mother too tired to consider new options. Job-site racial conflicts may preclude a union organizing campaign. Events going on in the environment around us may create new hope in our own situation, as did the sudden changes in Eastern Europe in 1989. And, conversely, perception of future possibilities can determine our strategic sense of what is possible in the now. It can even generate the enthusiasm with which the present task gets done. For example, prisoners with little hope of jobs upon release can hardly be interested in education or job-training programs.

Shaping the Present. The present, the time in which we live now, is first of all a product of the past. It is also shaped by our perceptions of the future. The people involved have specific histories which make or limit their present possibilities. For example, Congress and an administration which have created enormous national debt are not free to determine priorities or to fund new projects without regard to debt payments. Surprisingly, though, people's perceptions of the present is also partly a product of the future, especially of their expectations about that future. A few years ago, there was a lot of discussion about couples not having children because of their expectation of a nuclear war. Now a similar reaction is shaped by visions of deteriorating ozone layers, polluted water, economic projections, and overpopulation. Entire national policies and practices about births are determined in this cauldron of future-gazing.

A sense of this future orientation comes up very naturally when a young woman or man says, "I want to go to medical school; therefore I'm saving my money." The same kinds of future-implications are operative for many people, negative as well as positive. Many poor young women have so little expectations for their future that fear of unwanted pregnancy is negligible. Inner-city youth with little hope of surviving past twenty-five may seek immortality in siring children in or out of wedlock.

In a neighborhood where there is a lot of living life now and not worrying about the future, working for change takes on a new focus. The tenor of hopelessness in the present may require that we help to change the perceptions of future possibilities. We have to create the conditions and the capacity for imagination and creativity. Underlying that ability will be our own and our community's sense about how change is taking place. Is change gradual among folks we are working with? Or is it moving fast? Despite the publication of books like *Future Shock* and the release of movies like *Star Trek I, II, III, IV,* answering those questions again may be more a matter of intuition or temperament. Or, despite the possible objectivity in our analysis, our ability to accept the answers may be quite personal. It may depend on something so fundamental as the person's capacity for hope.

In effect, each of us has to make our own informed decision about the kind and pace of change and then try to fathom the sense of change in the environments around us. And the change we try to assess is also going on within ourselves, in others close to us, and on a neighborhood, national, and global scale. Such complexity about such an apparently simple thing as time is not intended to club us into passivity, but only to alert us to the many facets of what we call past, present, and future.

Finally, the particularized WHEN must be situated always within the larger scene. What takes place in my own neighborhood or community center reflects and is shaped by decisions being made at the state, national and international levels. What happens in the balance of trade, the flow of immigrants into this country, government tax policies at all levels, and the defense budget touches all of us. No one individual or organization operates in isolation. That may seem evident. Too often, though, fights that take place in a particular context and workplace frustrations get focused on one another when their causes and solutions are outside and beyond the local scene.

Personnel who endured the savaging of human services during the Reagan Administration can testify to tremendous frustrations created or radically intensified by decisions made in Washington. The causes were the slowdown and cutoff of funds, punitive legislation and regulations, and the threatened and real destruction of whole programs for the poor and homeless. These exacerbated already difficult working conditions for many in the non-profit sector and human services. This atmosphere soured many organizations, creating tension and conflict among workers.

On a larger scale, however, in Congress, state legislatures, United Way campaigns, and in church budget committees, it created tragic tensions over diminishing resources between those who feed the hungry and those who clothe the naked. Concerned decision-makers often found themselves making **triage** decisions among groups of poor, hungry, sick, or mentally disabled persons. While the individuals involved often could name the larger cause of problems, blame more often focused on those near at hand. In a practical sense, too, administrators caught up in survival struggles had little time for personnel development, conflict resolution, and other essentials of effective management. This is only one example of the importance of having a sense of the larger picture when asking the WHEN question. The need for that awareness prompts the next three questions about social reality.

WHERE

Asking this question—WHERE—even at the early information-gathering stage, reflects an expanded awareness about what is real. In addition to the WHO and WHAT of persons and things, social structures and institutions are concrete realities as well. Naming them helps to answer the question WHERE by clarifying the larger context in which we live and our multiple relationships with other people, things, and powers. And social structures expand our answer to the what-question by providing a three-dimensional profile of various institutions and entities.

Such structures are tough, hard-hitting, pervasive, and powerful facts that are essential to understanding all realities.[25] Understanding this insight takes us beyond the scriptures, beyond Jesus of Nazareth, and beyond the categories of thought of the apostolic church. For members of many religious movements and congregations, this new way of seeing and understanding was developed after their founder, their organization, and the formulation of their gospel-based mission. It is predominantly the insight of the twentieth century with the widespread development and acceptance of the social sciences.

The bottom line is that all of society is structured. It consists not just of individuals, machines, and commodities, but of organizations, structures, systems, and institutionalized "ways of doing things here." In the light of that insight, theologians have begun to speak a new language, unknown just a generation ago: "sinful social structures." Sinful and graced social structures have found a new currency in theological discourse. They convey that what is freeing, community-building, and love-generating (GRACE) and what is isolating, alienating, and destructive (SIN) is structured into social, cultural, political, and economic realities. Those structures, however, are not just "out there somewhere." They are internalized as profoundly held attitudes and values in individuals and groups.

The first part of the question WHERE focuses our viewer on what Holland and Henriot call the **objective dimension**[26] of social reality, which could be formal, legal institutions, associations, organizations, and behavior patterns. In any concrete situation of poverty, we must assess all the structures touching this situation. What works is more than an individual person acting as mayor, executive director, or community leader. Social analysis means asking: What is the role of the board in this institution, or the county commission? What is the job description of the housing authority director or head nurse? What corporation owns the local health care institution or food bank? What are the constraints built into its contracts?

In the **subjective dimension**, questions about social structures focus on what viewpoints, attitudes, and values are shaped and reinforced by this or that institution. How does the existence of a longstanding neighborhood organization, for example, determine how this community thinks about its garbage problem? How has it affected the sense of different individuals as leaders? This facet of analysis is often a two-way street, because socialized attitudes also support the existence and importance of these same organizations. Using the same example, how does the existence of this neighborhood organization limit the community's ability to think imaginatively about its options? Does it inhibit using other means to solve this problem?

In many communities, a factory was the critical institution in the development of the neighborhood. The neighborhood was built here because of the available jobs; family life developed around factory schedules; athletic teams were sponsored by union groups; and young people anticipated future employment in the pattern of their parents. As technology changes and industry scales back, closes, or moves, jobs begin disappearing. The infrastructure of the neighborhood begins disintegrating. Houses stand empty; nuclear families disappear; careers and dreams of employment are destroyed; and ultimately people's consciousness changes. Their self-value, the assumptions upon which they built their politics or prayed to God, their attitudes toward jobs and joblessness, and even their sense of past and future, all are transformed by changes in the community's dominant structure.

Informal institutions operate in any community as well. The brothel across from the office is a community institution. So too are gangs, sewing clubs, and the regular crowd at the spa. The analyst needs to ask, how does that institution function in this neighborhood? That is a question in the objective order. Related to it are the assumptions operating below the surface, as in formal structures: the relationships between women and men in this neighborhood; who can and cannot speak at a meeting; who will speak first or last because of assumptions about importance.

Analysis requires a closer look at institutions. Another way of asking the relational question, the WHERE, is to focus more closely on key institutions operative in the community, and how they affect people's lives. Institutions may be economic, political, cultural, religious, or social.

It is easy to begin with the **economic institutions**. We need to look at them individually, and in their interaction. What are the places of employment? What is the role of the factory? How does the welfare system, as an economic system, function? Is the welfare system, as a well-informed friend observed, "an economic support system from the government to large farmers and the upper class," providing survival supports to employees who work seasonally or to systematically under-paid domestics?

The next more obvious group are **political institutions**. We may easily identify the executive, legislative, and judicial branches at all lev-els of government. With them we may be able to name the political entities associated with political parties, the ward bosses, or their con-temporary equivalents. How do those institutions function in or over-against whatever agency, church, or neighborhood we are involved in? What are the professional associations, the unions, and the mer-chants' groups? How do they interact with elected officials and with the electoral process?

How is the **non-profit sector** organized? Sociologist Amitai Etzioni would distinguish three sectors of society: the private, the governmen-tal, and the "nongovernmental public sector, which encompasses sev-eral hundred thousand voluntary associations and corporations."[27] We often speak of this third sector as the non-profit sector, an extremely important factor in U.S. society and in social service and the promo-tion of social justice.

What does the United Way, for example, do in the community? The United Way fund-raising effort arose as a way to eliminate multiple col-lections and competition among non-profits. The precursor of the modern United Way was founded in Denver in 1887 by a Catholic priest, two Protestant ministers, and a rabbi; and many long-standing member agencies were founding partners of local United Ways else-where.[28] United Ways currently provide a process in which funding pri-orities are set and major community resources are collected and expended—a total of $1.9 billion in 1992. United Ways defend this as community-based, volunteer decision-making. Often these priorities are set, some critics say, on very traditional middle-class values, rather than social change and social advocacy agendas. Others, the long-stand-ing partner agencies, argue that United Ways are moving away from their historical responsibility to raise funds for the agencies that form the backbone of the community's response to social needs. Instead, they are increasingly responding to consumer choice pressures and interest groups competing for limited dollars. Thus, the allocation process is increasingly politicized.[29]

These criticisms suggest that there are a series of public or political choices being made through entities that we ordinarily do not think of as the public or governmental sector. The United Way is one such institution. In most of these nobody is publicly elected, but broad public policy is determined through the allocation of substantial community resources, both financial and professional. Activists must learn the variety of such non-profit entities, how they exercise their public functions, and how they interact with other institutions.

Often ignored, but very powerful, are the **cultural institutions** in any community. We may think immediately of the more formal museums, summer concerts, little theater, dance clubs, book groups, and wine tasting associations. The country clubs have long been powerful bastions of the rich and wealthy, where informal contacts and crucial community decisions occur.

The informal cultural structures are far more varied than might be imagined at first. Is there a lady who lives across the street from the parish church whose home everybody visits when they leave church? Who are the elders in this community? What is the role of the bar mitzvah or the debutante party as a community cultural institution? How do they function in socializing the young into society, in determining class status, in connecting new members of cultural elites to those who are in power? What are the racial, ethnic, religious, or other exclusions? Again, assessments have to consider original intents and purposes as well as the fully evolved institutions. One example would be the development in New Orleans' older Mardi Gras organizations from fanciful introductions of young women into adult society to highly structured entities reinforcing rigid racial and ethnic discrimination among members and guests.

The informal cultural institution may be a WHERE as well. My younger brother and his family now live in a rural area of Mississippi, where the former sheriff ran a popular downtown cafe. There, informal community decision-making, business connections, and just plain gossip takes place. In many such communities, there are corner stores, gas stations, and diners serving the same function of a cultural gathering place. Even more, they may function to initiate newcomers, nominate candidates, resolve disputes, and monitor community developments. Sorority and fraternity structures are locales where decisions are made, connections occur, and jobs are generated.

While many economic and political institutions have been subjected to laws regarding equal access over the past thirty years, cultural institutions often have been slow to open up. More well-known are country clubs and Mardi Gras organizations. Less well-known are single institutions such as the renowned Mory's in New Haven, the eating club and Yale's favorite meeting place. Mory's had been open to all Yale undergraduates until women were admitted in the late 1960s. Despite lawsuits and much unfavorable publicity, Mory's continued to exclude women for years.

The category of **religious or ecclesiastical institutions** includes both churches, mosques, and synagogues and the variety of social and human service institutions rooted in the faith communities. Much of the nation's voluntary health, welfare, education, and social services actually grew from these religious roots. Significant religious sponsorship remains. Religious institutions also include economic, political, and cultural elements. Since the vast majority of people in the United States identify themselves as believers, these institutions are critical to understanding most communities. How do they function in this civic community? What organizations work within the churches, and what non-church functions do they serve, for example, political or social purposes? No serious candidate seeking the black vote in most cities, for example, can avoid attending the black churches and even delivering some message. What functions do church leaders play in civic and political organizations?

Part of looking at the church-related institutions also involves, as discussed above, applying rigorous social, cultural, and historical analysis to those institutions to try to distinguish religious values, preaching, and practices from their acculturated embodiments. Such analysis is also used to better understand the ways in which the church itself as institution, including all its sub-institutions such as offices, laws, and organizations, is "culturally and historically conditioned."[30]

HOW

It is important also to look more deeply at social structures and institutions with a view to understanding their impact upon us. These are the many powerful ways in which they shape and influence people, policies, and societies. This helps us to answer the HOW question of local and national events.

Our HOW analysis first must look at **institutional faces**. Every institution has an outer and inner face. The first is shown to the world in the ways the institution acts in the external environment. This is easier to see. Organizations also have an internal face discerned initially in its organizational structures, decision-making modes, personnel policies, and the personnel themselves. Donal Dorr notes the importance of two corresponding ways in which organizations may be unjust: (1) "in what they do—e.g. exploiting the Third World, or depriving poor people of their rights, or charging excessive interest on loans"; and (2) "in the very way in which they are designed."[31]

Noting that both forms of structural injustice are common, Dorr spells out the inner structural injustice further:

> Secondly, there is an injustice built into the very way most of the large organisations in today's world are designed. They concentrate almost all power at the top; and that is itself an injustice, built into their structure; it deprives the ordinary workers of any effective control over the policies of the organisation in which they work.[32]

Dorr's point about internal injustice reflects the theme of subsidiarity in Catholic social teaching, where decisions in society should be made at the lowest effective level. He also underscores the point made in chapter one on burnout about the importance of shared decision-making within organizations, including, especially, those involved in social service and change advocacy and in the churches. Ways of examining the internal working of organizations include an **organic model** of social organization, which sees "growth and evolution happening through the harmonious and effective interrelationship of the parts," and a **social conflict model**, which "relies on conflict and division as the basic mode of organizational interaction."[33]

In analyzing Catholic social service agencies, Michael Maiello distinguishes three sociocultural models which influence organizational culture. The three models are **domesticating, corporate, and liberationist;** and they help us to better understand the HOW question even within these organizations. All organizations, he argues, develop their own systems of shared values and beliefs that produce norms of behavior. These systems constitute organizational cultures and are the faces they project to the world and recognize as their own. Organizational culture is produced by both internal dynamics and the surrounding environment. Efforts to reinforce or reform these cultures depend upon thoroughly understanding both these causal factors.

> Effective administrators know why and how their organization operates, and the extent to which it is influenced by external cultural models. Indeed, they realize that external influences from societal, behavioral,

philosophical, or theological models may be strong enough to mold and subsume administrators and organizations alike.[34]

Understanding organizational culture will enable those involved to strengthen the ability of institutions or agencies to develop their services consistent with their expressed values.

In the culture of domestication, Maiello explains, the organization works to preserve the status quo, seen as both necessary and valid. Those who succeed are the industrious, who are rewarded financially and valued by society. Persons with legitimate reasons for failing to compete or succeed are to be cared for by society, a role played by such organizations as Catholic social services. These agencies "provide for" people who are dependent, and social change efforts are discouraged. This cultural orientation affects choices of board members, management, and staff, promoting those who support existing policies. Advocacy for community empowerment, participative management, consultation involving needy persons themselves, and social justice advocacy are discouraged. Public relations and fund-raising focus on providing benevolent services within the existing order, and program development will tend to follow the dictates of funding sources rather than community needs.

The corporate culture manages limited resources in a cost effective manner to produce goods and services that will generate profit and growth. Valuing efficiency, competition, consumer choice, and entrepreneurial behavior, this type of organization is appealing in its effective management, program development, and service delivery systems. In the social sector, service is provided "to" persons in need who are "regarded as consumers or as members of designated target populations with needs that must be addressed programmatically."[35] Because this corporate culture values organizational growth to secure resources and enhance competition, the agency's resource allocation, program development, fund-raising, and public relations are focused on organizational purposes before people in need. Board members, management, and staff are valued for the benefits, resources, and expertise which they bring to the organization. Emphasis is on professionalism, efficiency, and effectiveness in management systems, fund-raising, and public relations. Programs are developed that promise increased funding or public relations benefits, not primarily to meet human needs and not to change society. When social change programs do exist, they are often underfunded and understaffed because they could threaten donors and funding sources. The organization's needs are primary.

The culture of liberation is focused on the dissent and reform that is an essential catalyst of change in U.S. history and present-day society. Built upon a primacy of human life, this culture's goals are eliminating poverty and oppression. This requires advocacy and social action in communion with the poor to change social structures causing poverty and to humanize society. In social agencies, according to Maiello, this culture results in two commitments: an inclusive "service with" needy persons; and personal and social empowerment. Agencies will value board members, management, and staff who are aware of the causes of social problems and committed to change. Boards and staff, in dialogue with persons in need, will be encouraged to initiate action in pursuit of goals. They will strive to eliminate injustice within the agency and to develop practices, including wages and benefits, that enhance human value and value human labor. Participative management, client involvement in needs assessment and program evaluation and planning, and empowerment will mark agency style. Public relations and development efforts will include education about injustices and remedial actions, and social justice advocacy will be integral.

Maiello concludes his analysis by insisting that, without advocacy and empowerment, social service agencies will be domesticated organizations and corporate entities concerned primarily with survival and growth. Even more importantly, without advocacy and empowerment, the church's mission of charity and justice and the welfare of the poor is in serious jeopardy. His point is important because, too often, especially in organizations that have grown up rapidly in the face of acute social needs or in response to funding opportunities, an analysis of the organization's own culture has never been made. Those within, however, especially those with an express interest in social justice and empowerment, will soon discern the injustices within and their connectedness to injustice in the larger world.

Looking inside institutions has a second meaning which goes deeper into its **animus**, its inner spirit. Using the scriptural "principalities and powers," Walter Wink comments:

> As the inner aspect they are the spirituality of institutions, the "within" of corporate structures and systems, the inner essence of outer organizations of power. As the outer aspect they are political systems, appointed officials, the "chair" of an organization, laws—in short, all the tangible manifestations which power takes. Every Power tends to have a visible pole, an outer form—be it a church, a nation, or an economy— and an invisible pole, an inner spirit of driving force that animates, legitimates, and regulates its physical manifestation in the world.[36]

Inside we find the powerful ways in which persons are shaped by institutions combined with a mythic power which transcends individuals and constitutes a literal institutional spirituality.

The suggestion of an inner spirituality to organizations brings with it a call to spiritual discernment of the inner life of institutions as part of our social analysis and theological reflection. Bill Kellermann argues, following Wink, that non-violent activists must combine discernment, rooted in Christian community, with their analysis. Both must be brought into play:

> The wider community of nonviolence has long held that a materialist approach to social change is naive, half-blind, and even "ineffective." We can change the leaders, we can oust the ruling class, we can seize the means of production, we can restructure the society, but if we haven't engaged a spiritual transformation, the new leaders and the new structures will be simply more of the same. As Ground Zero in Washington and other nuclear resistance communities say, "We must face the Trident submarine being put to sea, and we must face the Trident in our hearts."[37]

This insight into the inner and outer spirit underscores the importance of the WHY in social analysis, including consideration of powerful myths and symbols undergirding our social structures.

After looking at particular kinds of institutions, our analysis of relationships in social reality asks a further question. What are the **institutional alliances** among the various institutions?[38] Institutions do not exist or act alone, but analysis of their interaction is necessary to understanding HOW they affect us. For example, Amitai Etzioni points out that even the three so-called competing sectors—private, governmental, and non-governmental public—"are forever forming new amalgamations." He explains that government increasingly regulates the private sector, requiring it to shoulder more of the social costs of environmental protection and consumer safety. Etzioni also contends that "third-sector institutions" such as colleges and universities depend more now on government funds for scholarships, research, and loans. Thus, they are subject to leverage on hiring and enrollment of women and minorities.

The three sectors not only are amalgamated for various purposes, Etzioni adds, but they "interpenetrate." His first example comes from the health care field where government and voluntary mechanisms are mixed when review committees of doctors verify the need for certain services and hospital admissions of all Medicare and Medicaid (state funded) patients.[39] Other examples include the early U.S. alliance between economic and political power which imposed property requirements for voting rights. These alliances continue today, however, in Central America, where long-standing U.S. economic interests influenced both U.S. political and military policy there. How often, too, are decisions about state or federal prisons and hospitals determined by the economic and employment interests of the districts of key legislators? Asking about the connections, then, between the various kinds of institutions and interests is a more advanced and essential form of social analysis.[40]

One profoundly important form of social structure concludes this section, namely the **societal divisions**[41] running through much of the above. They were noted in simply determining WHO is involved in any situation. At this point we must underscore the positive and negative energy generated by the powerful ways we divide ourselves into races, classes, nationalities, gender, and other "isms." The analyst ignores these divisions only at great peril since, for example, race remains "one of the obsessive themes of American life"[42] and the women's movement is only now beginning to be felt. We then must ask repeatedly what societal divisions are at work? HOW are we divided in this institution or neighborhood and HOW do these groups interact?

Several years ago, I was in a group called Leadership Greater Baton Rouge, an annual community orientation program for thirty people from business, trade, industry, labor, the arts, and human services. By design, our group was one-third black, two-thirds white, and evenly divided between men and women. We broke for lunch during one of our monthly meetings, and went to an Italian restaurant nearby. When we split spontaneously into different carloads for the trip, even though various friendships and interest groups existed, we "naturally" divided by race.

Despite the best intentions at producing an integrated workforce, student body, or church parish, what happened in Baton Rouge that day too often happens. It has to do with how people get along and who people feel easy with. Those personal feelings, however, are so often a product of deeper historical societal divisions with, unfortunately, long futures. Those divisions have profound impact on social problems and their solutions. Race and skin color remain pivotal, but analysis must include ethnic groups, economic class, and religion.

WHY

When we ask WHY about social problems and conditions of injustice in our own society or worldwide, we enter the world of conscious and unconscious reasons, causes, motivations, benefits, profits, pay-offs, needs, and wants. Individuals and groups have reasons they can articulate and drives of which they are unaware. Institutions and organizations have publicly stated goals and objectives. They also have their own internal needs for growth, survival, legitimization, profit, and power.

Each kind of institution has its own underlying rationale and dominant drives, and there is often an entire field of the social sciences dedicated to the key structures, for example, economics. Economic institutions may be driven by profit maximization or by maximization of growth.[43] Rather than control by any identifiable person or group, in larger institutions, "control, motivation and goals are all deeply embedded and widely dispersed over the whole range of its managerial structure."[44] Self-interest, market forces, technological change, and corrective social mechanisms, such as government regulation, all contribute to the WHY of economic institutions.

Similar diversity exists in the WHY of politics and political institutions. Ego and altruism, lust for power and desire for service, social or religious commitment and varying ideologies, and consensus or conflict all play a hand in moving individuals and groups. Those with economic power tend to have political power as well. Those with power hold on to it and try to increase it; and they often succeed. Those without power tend to remain powerless. Power, Etzioni notes, is invested both within the government and in mobilized social groups, "cohesive aggregates of individuals acting in unison."[45]

Four factors, he adds, determine a social group's ability to make its viewpoint felt by government or other social groups:

> (1) the group's place in the stratification (or status) structure; (2) its degree of cohesion; (3) its level of mobilization; and (4) the allies with which it forms coalitions as compared with the opponents that coalesce against it.[46]

The lesson of this for the poor, as Saul Alinsky notes, is clear: "The only thing the poor have as far as power goes is their bodies."[47] To get what they need, Alinsky says, the poor have to organize "strong, militant organizations of their own."[48]

The WHY of culture is broader than particular formal and informal cultural institutions. Culture is about meaning, values, urges, and significance of ourselves, people around us, life and death, family, nation, and God. Some social activists have resisted the inclusion of the cultural as a major force in doing analysis. A year after the first edition of the Center of Concern's work on social analysis, author

Henriot underscored the importance of culture. While economic, political, and social structures are key, "it is culture which is the carrier of meaning and the shaper of values." To ignore culture or reduce it to a consequence of the economic or political, he wrote, is inadequate and misleading.[49] Francisco Ivern concurs, "Underneath socio-economic and socio-political structures there are some values which can be adequately analysed and explained only by study or analysis that is of a historical, philosophical, religious and cultural nature."[50]

Analysis must consider all elements of a society or a local community. Failure to attend to the cultural component may well doom the overall project. Ivern contends, echoing a point made earlier about the inner spirituality of institutions, that, even after radical political or social change,

> ...history demonstrates that these structural changes, even if radical, also leave intact certain more profound values (socio-cultural, socio-religious) which keep conditioning our way of thinking and acting, our relations with the world, with nature and with our fellow-beings.[51]

When the Holland-Henriot book was revised and expanded, the authors further explained their emphasis upon cultural elements in the face of excessively rational analysis and strategies, "The failure to grasp the creative role of rooted, passion-filled, meta-rational, collective symbols can be disastrous, countering the effectiveness of social change strategies."[52]

Cultural analysis must focus on the role of myths in social reality. These I will divide for this discussion into practical myths particular to specific organizations or groups and thematic myths with a deeper and more universal influence. Understanding a community's myths is critical to understanding its culture.

> Myths are stories human communities tell about themselves to convey the distinctive meaning of their world—or their world view. These myths show the presuppositions which set the boundaries of the group's identity and of their judgments of their life and action. Because myths create a symbolic world that appeals to the whole person, to emotion and imagination, as well as to reason, they evoke the vicarious participation of the community. Both consciously and unconsciously a people's myths influence their behavior.[53]

Myths are central to social analysis. They, more than any other cultural component, legitimize social and economic structures, including those which create injustice, poverty, and war. Here we can cite the

Aryan racial myths that fueled Nazi Germany's extermination of Jews, Poles, persons with mental disorders, and many others, or the manifest destiny myth that buttressed our own government policies resulting in the genocide of Native peoples.

Practical myths are those which operate in the context of specific organizations or communities. They say something to us about ourselves, about people across the tracks, or about the larger city. The practical myth also may operate in the social agency, community group, church parish, or other institutions concerned about changing social realities. Activists need to look to their own working group to discern whether it is in fact accomplishing its purposes. Sometimes, as with the sequoias in California, our own organization may have strayed from its original intent and even be contributing to community problems.

In law school, for example, we learned that there were four classic reasons for prisons: (1) they punished offenders for their crimes; (2) they restrained those imprisoned from committing additional crimes; (3) they rehabilitated inmates to lead a crime-free life after incarceration; and (4) they deterred other people from committing the same or similar acts. If we think prisons are doing those four things, then we should spend money to do that, imprison people for their crimes, or release people because of their rehabilitation. But past decades have raised this question about our prisons: does what we think we are doing really happen in these institutions?[54] If not, why bear the enormous expenditure, inflict the human cost, and simultaneously watch the crime rate rise? Similar questions are asked about our school, welfare, and health care systems.

Our **thematic myths** tap us into those deeper, broader stories or images that cut across different societies and cultures. Like racism and sexism, "they are charged with emotional power and tend to organize other images in the human imagination."[55] In social injustice and war making, powerful myths operate with devastating impact. These include myths of racial or gender superiority, the correlation of wealth and moral uprightness or poverty and divine disfavor, and national manifest destiny.

Three particular kinds of myths are worth noting here. The first are the myths underlying dominant economic systems. Donal Dorr explains in the context of Western capitalism:

> But capitalism has another face, a more attractive one. It is what might be called "frontier free enterprise," typified in the small-town entrepreneurs who use local resources and their own initiative and skill to meet local needs and provide employment....The idealised image of free

enterprise is used to give respectability to capitalism in its less accept-able forms. Frequently this takes place unconsciously, simply because people have not had the opportunity or education to make the neces-sary distinctions. But it is not at all uncommon to have a deliberate manipulation, a campaign to justify capitalism in its more unacceptable forms through a glamorisation of the ideal of free enterprise.[56]

Similar mythology has been used in support of socialist models of eco-nomic organization. One such myth has developed from the story of the sharing of goods among the early apostolic Christian communities idealized in the pages of the Acts of the Apostles.

A second powerful set of myths operate in the realm of the family, the center of most social organizations. Myths operate to sustain and support family life, intergenerational responsibilities, and family roles. Maria Riley explains a dominant myth about women's familial responsibility:

> Cultural, social and religious values converge in creating the myth that women are more responsible for the quality of family life than men. This pervasive attitude places overwhelming burdens on the woman worker throughout the world. She is not only often overworked and underpaid in the work place; she is also expected to carry the primary tasks of homemaking and child care. Few countries or industries assume any responsibility for providing social policy and programs to alleviate this burden. In fact, more often women are penalized when the demands of their family or maternity leave interfere with production.[57]

While these myths apply directly to social organizations such as the family, they obviously have wide ranging economic impact.

For those concerned about violence and war-making, a third area of myth-making arises about those who are different from ourselves. Donald Gelpi explains about the myth of "The Others":

> We generalize all too easily about the attitudes, beliefs, values, and life-style of groups to which we do not belong. Such generalizations fre-quently do no harm; but when sadistic bigotry hardens them into stereotypes, social generalizations begin to teem with violent possibili-ties. We confront the members of unfamiliar social groups as The Others. Historically, we humans have dealt with threats posed by The Others in a variety of ways. We have tried to denigrate, avoid, isolate, or eliminate The Others (as Hitler did to the Jews in Germany and as Americans have attempted to do to blacks and other races of color in this country). Or we have tried to assimilate The Others into familiar social roles (as WASP America did to European immigrants). Or we can

accommodate to The Others and through a process of mutual adjust-
ment work out a social arrangement mutually acceptable to both....
Finally, we can identify with The Others in their otherness, as liberation
theologians demand that affluent Christians do with the poor.[58]

These myths about our differences are very powerful, operating in
every neighborhood and nation. In their extreme destructive form,
these myths transform others into what Gerard Vanderhaar calls
"Enemy," a concept evoking fear, hostility, and even war.[59]

The power and widespread impact of these myths remind us that
there is a responsibility to **demythologize the social agenda**. We must
discern and disclose all those myths which are not only false but
destructive of the fundamental concerns for giftedness, stewardship,
and human community. This is one more instance of the importance
in social ministries of unmasking the realities lurking behind the legiti-
mation of social structures.[60]

At the same time, there is a commensurate concern that we recognize the power of existing religious and social myths that promote justice and peace. When they are found in a particular situation, we
should work to accentuate and develop them. Where such myths are
lacking or too weak, it will be important to **remythologize the social
agenda** with powerful images. These include creation, stewardship,
covenant community, the **anawim**, jubilee, social and racial equality,
hope, liberation, solidarity, the reign of God, and **faithjustice**. This is
a uniquely appropriate task for people committed to justice and
peace, especially effective in the hands of teachers, parents, story-
tellers, media specialists, politicians, and preachers.

Without extensive consideration here, it is important as well to
note the distinct role played in the cultural sector by the use of **symbol and language**. Like myth, symbols powerfully convey meaning in
support of justice or injustice, graced or sinful patterns of behavior
and structures. Included may be the powerful national symbols of
"flag, faith, and family,"[61] the status symbols of automobiles and attire,
or the "symbols of identification" of clothing or hairdo.[62] Symbols
such as the peace sign, the raised and clenched fist, the flag, the femi-
nine ♀, the farmworker black eagle, and the victory "V" have carried
powerful meanings in recent social and political history. They also are
susceptible to manipulation and exploitation for injustice, especially in
our media and image dominated society.

Specific language-uses also reveal hidden realities, attitudes, and
power relationships. They, too, may be manipulated for political purposes, e.g., calling the opposition forces in Nicaragua either "contras"

or "freedom fighters" in order to convey wide ranges of meaning. President Reagan was extremely adept at this in a sound-bite society. His use of "truly needy," for instance, subtly distinguished some of the poor from an untold number of poor persons who were somehow to blame for their condition and therefore not deserving of compassion or assistance. This usage reinforced American bigotry against the poor and Reagan's own devastating budget cutbacks in domestic programs. As the 1992 presidential race again reminded us, politics in America has been increasingly reduced to "sound bites." The seven-second visual that is honed to carry a wealth of meaning has effectively replaced serious political discourse. This kind of politics evokes more passion or prejudice than fact or reality. We are all poorer for this development, but it underscores the power of symbol and language in human society.

In contrast, Etzioni contends that language changes, "for example, calling blacks 'blacks,' rather than 'Niggers,' or women 'women' rather than 'girls,' 'chicks,' or 'broads,' indicates at least a measure of acceptance of the values involved."[63] I would add that the tactical promotion in business, home, media, or liturgy of changes involving sexist language raises consciousness in two ways. It highlights the underlying issues involved in gender discrimination, women's rights, and equal work; and it also underscores the inherent dignity of women themselves.

Then, finally, after the WHO, WHAT, WHEN, WHERE, HOW and WHY, we again focus on the three Holland-Henriot questions related to class: "Who makes the decisions?" "Who benefits from the decisions?" and "Who bears the costs of the decisions?" These questions apply currently to labor-management relations, where we are "rebuilding America" and readjusting for a leaner economy. And they are equally applicable to local decisions about rezoning, relocating the community high school, and spending Community Development Block Grant funds to beautify the town square.

Answering these questions lays the foundation for doing theological reflection, for value-based judgments of what we have analyzed which then leads us to act. This is the long way around to the point made by the synod of bishops in Rome in 1971 that action for justice is a constituent element of preaching of the gospel.[64] Ultimately that is what we do in social analysis and in the Pastoral Circle: moving from faith-filled reflection on human social reality to action for a more just society.

In conclusion, it should be clear just how powerful social analysis is in the hands of the activist. It is more powerful, as well, when done with coworkers and especially with persons who are poor and vulnerable. It is only they who can offer us new perspectives that free us to see the world honestly.

The problems around us are critically important; human lives and happiness are at stake; and the misery which engulfs so many millions of people cannot but touch the compassionate heart and move us to act. That is the imperative which has prompted the intense and urgent calls to action from the church over the past thirty years. Effectively responding requires taking the time to prepare ourselves individually by education, work experience, and the schooling in human compassion that is only learned from face-to-face contact with persons in need. It also requires the kind of time-consuming and careful analysis proposed here by individuals, groups, governments, and churches. If we search for perfect knowledge and perfect planning, however, to guarantee our success, we will be dead before we feel free to act.

No matter how daunting the task of analyzing social reality may seem, the fact is that such analysis is going on constantly—by others and within our own minds and hearts. The challenge here is consciously and reflectively to do analysis so that what we truly intend on behalf of justice and peace is what we actually do.

CHAPTER THREE

Out of the Darkness

We're talking about **a certain kind of interiority, a certain kind of community**. We're talking about communities of resistance, of inner struggle, that recognize in themselves the impact of social sin, if you want, and struggle against it. And that's what brings them together.... So it's a kind of interiority that we are interested in, **a kind with its face towards the world**, judging the sin of the world and announcing the Kingdom of God.

JOSEPH P. DAOUST, S.J.
1981 SOCIAL MINISTRIES DIALOGUE[1]

New Haven law school days were marked by war and racism. Speeches, marches, and demonstrations focused on the Vietnam War, including the invasion of Cambodia. Racial issues were primed by the Black Panther trial and a major demonstration that turned from peaceful to violent partly by a premature order to mobilize the national guard. What bothered me most about both sets of events, at least within the world of the law school and law student gatherings was the absence of any real dialogue on the issues involved and the controlling dominance of a few self-appointed leaders or spokespersons.

* * *

My second year in theology studies began with a weekend away in the country for my community of twelve. We had decided to tell our personal and family stories as a way to improve our relationships and strengthen the bond among us for the year. Early on, one of the participants openly told us of his past emotional traumas, including hospitalizations. In so doing, his honesty triggered the most frank and caring group exchange I had ever experienced. It was as if his personal freedom had liberated each of us to reveal aspects of ourselves and our histories which had been bottled up for years. The foundation of that weekend together allowed us to honestly and compassionately address a wide range of personal and community questions during the year. These included specific decisions to simplify our community lifestyle, something which had eluded the best efforts of other groups with whom I had lived.

* * *

My experience with the Jesuit Volunteer Corps (JVC) as a board member and trainer began with the founding of its southern branch in 1979 and has continued to the present. The JVC is now the largest full-time Catholic lay volunteer organization in the U.S., numbering more than five hundred women and men working in social and pastoral settings among the poor from Alaska, where it was founded in 1956, to Florida. JVC formulates its goals in terms of four key elements: (1) social service and advocacy; (2) simple lifestyle; (3) community life; and (4) a commitment to spiritual development of its members. These volunteers live in small "simple lifestyle" communities among the poor, work in a variety of organizations and situations, and try to nurture both a community and personal spiritual depth. I have always been inspired by their struggles to maintain these four goals.

* * *

Thirty-six of us, evenly divided between women and men and one-third black and two-thirds white, comprised the 1987 Leadership Greater Baton Rouge class. On this one of our monthly days together, the focus was on race and gender. After preliminary considerations, the afternoon session began with an exchange of our "stories" of formative experiences of racism and sexism.[2] We were divided into smaller groups for convenience. One after another developed the sinews of their journey in tales of personal and family heroism, pain, dreams, struggles, failures, tears and laughter. Only then did we begin to understand much of what had been said and unsaid in preceding months of meeting together on various civic issues. You might say that we were learning to read between the lines. This one session alone did more to bond us together as a class than all other events in the year-long program.

If the use of the Pastoral Circle—insertion, analysis, reflection, and action—is effective, it should bring us to new levels of insight into our experiences and our work. It should also lead us to new ways of doing things. Social analysis should provide us with the understanding and insights that allow us to see better what enhances and what undermines the values we pursue, for example, stewardship and the development of covenant community.[3] In this way social analysis bridges us into theological reflection. This theological reflection is not the prerogative of a few professional theologians, but it is a "reflective exercise of faith"[4] which should be taking place wherever believing people encounter world realities.

Just such an experience occurred for me in a two-year long process of reflection with a dozen others who comprised the National Board of Jesuit Social Ministries. It is this experience that lays the foundation for this chapter. Each of us was charged with responsibility for promoting work for **faithjustice** in various parts of the country. As a group, we directed the advocacy and service work of the staff of our national social ministries office in Washington, D.C. In the group were writers, educators, lawyers, community organizers, missionaries, economists, pastors, and administrators. We met together for the better part of a week two or three times a year in various parts of the country.

In a several-year evolution, the board decided that our own method of meeting together should include a number of interwoven factors. We would not only have business and working sessions, but if possible in each locale, there would be time set aside for prayer together, personal narratives and mutual support, preparation and clean-up of our meals, and recreation and relaxation. Critical to our way of proceeding as well were meeting sites in places close to urban poverty and visits with poor persons and those working with them in such local poverty settings as neighborhoods, jails, and housing projects. We were convinced that our own ability to move as a group through personal and structural resistances to peace and justice would be enhanced by deepening our mutual trust. That, in turn, could only be done by a range of shared experiences, support, challenge, and insights, especially the common contact with the poor.

Then, in the early 1980s, we embarked on a process of looking more in depth at three specific advocacy priorities which had been established several years earlier: Native American issues, Hispanic concerns, and what we called "arms/peace." We determined that our consideration of each question should be done in a specific context, namely where people were gathered or focused on these efforts. For us, this meant going to San Antonio to examine the Hispanic concern, to Seattle for arms/peace, and meeting with the Catholic Native American Tekawitha Conference in Denver.

We planned that our examination of each priority issue should be a combination of preparatory reading, shared experiences, and discussion with persons involved. In each location, there would be some specifically planned, however brief, insertion experience. By this we meant an eyes/hands/heart exposure to the "stuff" of the issue. This meant spending time with peace activists at the Ground Zero anti-nuclear center outside the Trident base near Seattle. We also visited jails, community organizations and housing projects in San Antonio. And we attended song, prayer, dance, and discussions with the Native Americans gathered in Denver. Despite some artificiality, these planned experiences were intended to open us up to more than just intellectual analysis, to put faces and features on the issues, and to enflesh considerations about what we could do back home or in the national office on priority concerns.

These disparate experiences actually involved each of the four moments of the Pastoral Circle. From insertion among the people and exposure to their issues came analysis and reflection. These in turn were designed to help us to develop action at both the regional and national levels. The process worked effectively for us through the year or more during which we moved from San Antonio to Denver to Seattle.

These concerns subsequently led us to ask a further question, "What are the connections between the issues; what is happening in the larger context of the United States that encourages us as a nation to spend enormous sums on implements of war while poor and minority children do not have enough to eat, decent health care, or hope for the future?" The context for asking that question was the site chosen for our next meeting: the South Bronx. There we met in a neighborhood that literally looked like a battle zone.

In the Bronx we again took up the three issues of Hispanics, Native Americans, and arms/peace. This time, however, we addressed these three concerns with a specific question, "How do the things we have seen and reflected on during the past two years connect to one another?" "What are the underlying forces that are common to the people we met in various places which shape their lives even in these different environments?" To ask these questions honestly, though, we found we had to look inside ourselves, our own families and local communities, our religious communities, and at the world around us. We were looking at all the levels, sectors, or dimensions of society—at what Michael Crosby calls the "individual, interpersonal, and infrastructural."[5]

Because of who we were, we particularly asked what was happening in the personal, family, and community lives of those working in these very communities of concern we had visited. What was happening especially among those trying to change the structures that oppress one group or another or that build war instead of peace. In Ignatian and scriptural language, we moved into theological reflection asking where were light and darkness. These are traditional discernment terms that suggest the movement of God's grace and Spirit or, on the contrary, the blocking of God's activity by the forces of sin and evil.

The WHEN of our conversations was the early Reagan years and the context was his tremendous cutbacks in domestic social and human service programs coupled with awesome escalation of defense spending. For those working among the poor and for poor communities, this was the beginning of a period of widespread acute darkness and heart-rending disappointment. Since then new hopes have been generated for investment in the problems of poverty and racism in America through a "peace divided" to be found from the end of the Cold War. Those hopes, however, have been shattered in turn by the bailout of the Savings and Loans, a new war in the Gulf region, and a crushing deficit. Because of those and other developments the darkness and disappointment of the eighties has certainly spilled over into the nineties. Much of this group's insights then remain extremely valid for me today.

Three Dimensions of Darkness

We asked the darkness question first, and we focused it upon the larger social, economic, and political scene. This was the first of the three dimensions examined. "When we look at the world around us, what do we see of darkness? What are the contours of the dark side?" Our discussions soon turned up a list of six dominant themes which we found recurring in the experiences of minority groups, the poor, and our militarized culture:

SOCIAL-ECONOMIC-POLITICAL DARKNESS

1. Systemic and destructive competition among classes, races, and nations.
2. Seeing others as "them."
3. Exploitation of the poor.
4. Marginalization of "non-productive" groups.
5. Tremendous waste of human and environmental resources.
6. Violence and an epidemic of arms building and arms sales.

The first consistent theme at the systemic level was competition, a destructive competition for power, resources, and status among classes, races and nations. At the national level, for example, the Administration's 1981 budget made it clear that the nation could not afford to, or was unwilling to, simultaneously take care of its domestic needs, cut taxes for the wealthy, and engage in the largest peacetime military spending increase ever. It was classic guns or butter thinking. The losers were the poor and the minorities for whom poverty has been an intractable foe. Related, too, was perceived competition between the races for supposedly limited economic resources and jobs, for political power in the cities, and for neighborhood control. And as a backdrop to all this was the great and destructive competition between us as a nation and the U.S.S.R., primarily in terms of the arms race, but dressed up at the Olympics or in the space race.

The second dark side phenomenon was seeing other people as "them," the application of the myth of "The Others" described in chapter two. Go to the Southwest, and the "them" is the substantial Hispanic or Native American population. "They" are not like us, be they Russians, Hispanics, poor people, or Native Americans. In the late seventies and early eighties, during the famous hostage crisis, our political and media establishments made a special effort to paint the Iranians as "them." In the early nineties, we turned the people of Iraq into "them" and devastated their armies and their civilian infrastructure in a war now seriously questioned by a majority of the U.S. population. Once people are painted as "them," then they are deemed to be so unlike ourselves that bigotry, economic and social discrimination, and even violence against them are justifiable.

The third area of systemic darkness was exploitation of the poor. We use up the poor in a variety of ways that we are often unaware of. Their labor often performs the most menial tasks and services, usually for the lowest possible wages. Their votes are thought to be saleable for the right political promises. The homeless sell their own blood to just get through another day. The neighborhoods of the poor are often used for locating undesirable plants or dumping toxic wastes. And even their bodies are the staples of medical school laboratories and medical education.

The fourth pattern we saw was marginalization of non-producers. Many of the elderly, Native Americans, and Hispanics, for example, cannot or do not "produce" in the system, at least not in our traditional market economy. They are marginalized, pushed to the fringe of society. Many of the poor are not, in economic terms, particularly useful. The same thing would apply to persons with disabilities, to welfare mothers, and to a lot of other groups looked down upon in this and other societies. They are "culturally unfit."

Related to this is the horrible waste of resources both human and environmental. This fifth area of darkness can be seen in, for example, widespread unemployment and alcoholism in the Native American community. It also is reflected in the dropout rates for minority children in schools across the nation. And it is most evident in the diversion of the goods of the earth into nuclear weapons, whose only use can be total human and environmental destruction.

Finally, the dark side revealed the issue of violence and arms building. The Middle East, Northern Ireland, Central America, South Africa, Southeast Asia and the devastation of so many other places testify to this theme. Violence occurs in conflict between the races, seen most recently in police brutality and mob looting and burning in Los Angeles. It also is manifest in the prevalence of suicide in the Native American community. And, writ large, violence reigns in our hearts in the readiness of this whole society to inflict widespread horror on the entire world in its mutually-assured-destruction (MAD) nuclear weapons policy. With it, of course, goes the real violence done by defense spending upon the sick, poor, homeless, uneducated, and needy of this society and the world. Their basic needs could be met with only a portion of what is spent on arms and armaments.

After reviewing these key themes of darkness in the social-structural sector, we then focused a little closer to home. "What darkness do we see at the interpersonal level, in the communities of people working for justice, among our own families and friends, within poor communities, in church parishes, or among religious congregations?" Again, from among a number of issues and concerns a short list of six dominant themes was drawn up:

INTERPERSONAL OR COMMUNAL DARKNESS

1. Violence in families, groups, and neighborhoods.
2. Intolerance of "others."
3. Competition for renown, male-female competition, use of others in relationships.
4. Lack of fidelity.
5. Loss of shared vision.
6. Lack of investment in groups or relationships.

On Easter Sunday afternoon in 1992, the doorbell rang in our center city Washington community. When I opened the door, four young children holding hands in our front yard chanted, "Happy Easter, Mr. Priest." Not everyone in this predominantly black neighborhood knows what to call us, but the sentiment was friendly and delightful. After a brief conversation with the young people about their family Easter celebrations, one child remarked that he and his sister were moving to their grandmother's in North Carolina. As they were walking back down the street I called out, "North Carolina is a beautiful place." He responded back over his shoulder, "And they don't kill people there either."

Neighborhoods of the poor are often centers of social violence, our first theme in this examination of darkness in the second sector of society. Interpersonal violence is all too common in the American family, too. In Baton Rouge, Catholic Community Services sponsored a workshop program in the mid-eighties bringing together specialists in spouse abuse, child abuse, and elder abuse. While the effort to examine the connections between these three epidemics was only a beginning, it highlighted themes of frustration, the exercise of power over the less powerful, and the need to teach people new ways to deal with conflict and tension. There is simply too much violence in U.S. neighborhoods and cities. Our romance with guns, camouflaged beneath First Amendment rhetoric, only exacerbates the problem.

At this interpersonal level, our group also noticed an intolerance of "others." By this we meant the refusal to grant to people different from ourselves the same rights and privileges which we enjoy. "They" do not experience the same needs and desires as we do and certainly cannot have the same values. This is similar to the operation of the "them" phenomenon in the public sector. Only now this exclusivity manifests itself at the neighborhood school, on the job site, in the community church. Racism is one form of this intolerance between people who have differences. The relationship between heterosexual and homosexual is another good example. Tensions and misunderstanding can exist, however, between those whose only apparent difference is between introversion and extroversion. Persons with HIV/AIDS would also be more recent victims of this kind of alienation.

We next noted the competition and exploitation which occurs in relationships, especially in interpersonal relationships between men and women. Women in the white collar or blue collar workplace can tell many stories about the experience of being perceived as threat by men and about being treated as anything but coworkers. Sexual exploitation, once hidden, has become the topic in U.S. Senate confirmation hearings and widespread investigations into the behavior of naval officers. This kind of competition and exploitation, however, reaches far beyond gender relationships. A poignantly frustrating and aggravated form of competition had been created among those working for social justice by Reagan budget cuts in the early 1980s. Suddenly, motivated by the same desire to help those in need, people who fed the hungry were fighting people who clothed the naked for diminishing public dollars. And escalating social needs and declining federal involvement increased competition within the private sector, such as in local United Way allocation processes. There, people who housed the homeless found themselves fighting those who cared for the sick, all for the same limited dollars. It was competition in its most perverse form, a tragedy of immense proportions; but it was real. This competitiveness continues today as social needs continue to grow, the economy stagnates, and federal tax and spending policies squeeze existing programs.

The fourth interpersonal theme of darkness was a lack of fidelity, an increasing reality in marriages and in religious congregations. This factor also was evident in groups working on social issues and in communities committed to social change. For some, their exodus from the struggle for justice and peace related directly to the massive amputations in the federal domestic budget and the ensuing atmosphere of despair. We also believed that defections from social change work also reflected deeper societal themes of individualism and lack of commitment.

Even among those who remained in marriages, families, churches, and groups committed to social justice, we found a loss of shared vision. The days of Dr. Martin Luther King, Jr. were over; the stirring speeches were gone. No one marched on Washington in the numbers or with the vitality of days past. The vision which could galvanize the loyal and move the uncommitted seemed something for TV's "remember when" and the museums. This absence was noted specifically among people working among the poor, among church people, and, of course, in our national leadership. Even Mr. Reagan, while topping the charts in personal popularity, did not really mold a genuine national consensus on critical issues in a decade of me-first politics. President Bush even later disclaimed "the vision thing...."

A final darkness theme was the lack of genuine investment expended on behalf of worthwhile causes and people in need. This condition seemed to haunt even good people who continued to work for social justice, church, neighborhood, or peace. The daily work of meetings, newsletters, and "actions," the community organizer's bread and butter, continued. Much of it, however, did not go much past the office or the church door. The timeclock, paycheck, or tenure seemed more to the point than genuine social or community change.

Moving to the personal level, we then asked ourselves, "What darkness is going on in within ourselves, within people working for social justice, and others in ministry? What drives, desires, motives, and fears do we experience within ourselves and other contemporaries committed to the same values and the same work?" We also considered the patterns of personal development or regression in the larger society. Again, some hours of animated conversation yielded another short list of central themes or trends:

PERSONAL DARKNESS

1. Loneliness and escapes from it.
2. Fears: of failure, of others, of ourselves, and of new ventures.
3. A sense of powerlessness before extrinsic forces, fatalism.
4. Excessive consumption.
5. A lack of intrinsic worth.
6. No real relaxation or recreation, drivenness, and burnout.

In the sphere of personal darkness, we found loneliness prevalent among a number of people with whom we lived or worked in social justice ministries or in the church. The prominent way of relating to that loneliness was not confrontation with it. People seemed unwilling to understand its causes or cures, to take the personal and even spiritual means to respond. Instead their lives seemed to be filled more with an unending and creative number of ways of trying to escape from loneliness, including both excessive consumption and excessive work, both discussed below.

Secondly, many people seemed obsessed with a number of fears. Some feared failure most of all, a characteristic found even among those in service to the poor or advocacy for a more just society. Even well-intentioned people seemed to really fear others with whom they lived and worked. This fear showed itself especially in terms of resisting or avoiding deep-felt relationships requiring that they engage themselves with others, opening themselves up to share their own person and risking vulnerability. Some of us seemed to fear even our own real selves. Others, even those who had already stepped out in solidarity with the poor, still had a fear of new ventures, of taking new risks, of trying new ways of doing things, especially in the area of social justice.

In some ways, the fears seemed related to a third area of personal darkness. This was the sense of powerlessness before extrinsic forces, and before life and death. There seemed an almost palpable sense that life finally had beaten us. This expressed itself in a fatalism that proclaimed, "There is nothing you can do that really matters, especially in the face of the immense decisions made in Washington." This was reflected in those who saw the social justice task and the call of the church to it as too monumental to grasp.[6] Moreover, people who actually had been in the trenches of the battle for racial and social justice since the King days did not find things to be all that much better fifteen years later. Their efforts seemed fruitless, doomed to be swallowed up by larger forces and dominant apathy. Now, ten years still later, police brutality and riots in Los Angeles are only one vivid reminder that widespread social problems persist, adding to the sense of frustration among those long committed to social change.

Excessive consumption seemed more to be the order of the day. Food, clothes, alcohol, TV, mechanical devices, and shopping centers full of distractions only seem to whet our appetite for consumption, another aspect of personal darkness. We seemed to create a cushion of comfort to escape from loneliness and experiences of, or even the risk of, failure. People spent more and more money on stereos, cars, Izod shirts, booze, places to eat and be seen eating, movies, and so forth. In ten years the fashions have changed but not the fact of U.S. consumerism, now exported to much of the world. It was as if these possessions or even the accumulation of exciting experiences could somehow blunt our awareness of terrible societal inequities seemingly resistant to solution.

Too many people around us seemed overwhelmed by a lack of intrinsic self-worth, another piece of the personal darkness. They were without that sense, rooted in Genesis itself, of their own goodness, dignity, and purposefulness. They could not believe they were created good in God's own image. Without the God within and around them, they were seeking self-value in the American way: in grades and degree programs, credentials, and salaries. This is a lesson drilled into us from our first standardized test, when the great question was what percentile we had scored in. In this culture, we learn early that the 85th percentile makes us better than 85 percent of our contemporaries. We are weaned now on this kind of comparative externalized value from late elementary school, as we are subjected to our first national standardized exam. Standardized self-valuing stays with us through college boards, admission exams for graduate schools, law schools, medical schools, and for the professions.

Lastly, especially among those working for a more just society, we found no real relaxation, no real recreation. Too many were consumed with just pushing on, a drivenness that sanctions no withdrawal from the battle. No quarter is given, and no retreat allowed. They were burned out.

The Engines of Darkness

Our conversation then took another turn as we looked at the central themes of darkness operative at the individual, communal, and systemic levels. The three dimensions of intertwined reality prompted this question, "Are there any common themes, looking at these three, that cut across them all?" We were seeking multidimensional connections. Upon further analysis and reflection, five major darkness themes predominated. I call them "the engines of darkness." They comprised critical forces which were all operative in the experience of reflecting upon society, upon the communities of people working among the poor, and upon ourselves. In each case, there may be positive aspects of a theme, but our reflection was focused then on the dark side of reality, seeing these factors in their excessiveness, their destructive capacity in us and our society.

COMPETITION

The first pervasive multilevel theme was **competition**. Especially under the influence of our economic system, so much of our personal self-value, our sense of intrinsic worth as Americans, is tied up in production and in comparing our own production with that of others. In the socioeconomic sphere, it profoundly shapes our attitudes especially toward the non-productive poor and marginalized. Thus, we negatively assess the elderly, welfare mothers, and the chronically unemployed in the United States. This attitude also influences our stance toward third world nations, viewed not as producers but as sources of raw materials and consumer markets for our products.

This competitiveness even affects people involved in social ministry in the subtle competition between those in parallel services such as food banks, disability agencies, and legal services. The more insidious attitudes of distrust arise between those who engage in service work and those committed to advocacy. To service providers, advocates can seem detached from real people and their needs, more interested in causes than concern. To advocates, service workers can appear to be engaged in short-sighted "band-aid" work that only ameliorates the damage the system does, without changing the structures before they injure more persons.

In the communitarian sector, Rosine Hammett and Loughlin Sofield observe that all groups experience the development of a hierarchy of members. This occurs first when the "membership usually arranges itself on a continuum of least important to most important." The criteria may vary from academic degrees to verbal ability. "Competition is fierce, and the threat to each person's sense of self-worth is great."[7] In particular, gender-competition shapes behavior toward men or women, fed by more traditional personal differences and now the politicizing of feminist and anti-feminist movements. We likewise tend to harbor misunderstandings and resentments toward the elderly or the young, toward those who cannot carry their weight in our household or workplace, and ultimately toward those who are different from ourselves.

Within ourselves, competitive drivenness has affected our self-value since they handed out the first gold stars in kindergarten, the A's in school, and college admission scores. We measure ourselves by the size of our biceps, automobiles, and salaries. According to Dean Brackley, the dominant metaphor for our human community is the **ladder**:

> Under these conditions, competition characterizes social life. One's security is threatened, principally by others. The neighbor below me threatens not only my material and social security but my value as a human being. The neighbor above devalues me and is threatened by me. Social relations are based, not on mutuality and trust, but on the fear and defensiveness that seeks security through force, deterrents, multiple door locks, pistols, and attack dogs. To control my life I have to control my world.[8]

In many social transactions, the imperative is to create winners and losers, not partners and colleagues. Even among those engaged in the same enterprise of charity or justice, we may find ourselves basing our own self-esteem on the implied competition of relative caseloads, community recognition, advancement within the agency, or who works longest and latest and, therefore, is most committed to the poor.

DOMINATION

What results is further and further competition, aggression and violence at home and in politics, workaholism, and white and blue collar property crimes in pursuing the compulsive societal creed that "more is better." It is the ultimate search for winning, for **domination**, the second major engine of darkness. Put another way, we have to be in control, in charge. Our self-value and our value in personal relations and in international relations is only secure in dominance and control. "If I'm in charge," I say to myself, "nothing can go wrong. If I have to share power with somebody else, I can never be sure what will happen." Brackley ties this directly to our fundamental insecurity:

> Today we walk about **less secure** and **more anxious**—as individuals, communities, and nations—in the face of the dangers of nature and the uncertainties of history and society; we are **more alone**, as well. Small wonder that a striving for certitude and predictability suffuses our culture or that we appeal to science and technology to guarantee them. The temptation to self-sufficiency has led us modern individuals to try to control our lives and the world around us. In our century of total war, totalitarianism, and nuclear weaponry, this **hubris** has taken on breathtaking, and catastrophic, proportions. The modern individual has indeed become the autonomous, God-less individual. We have come to try to solve the insecurity of life more and more by ourselves, without God—and without others.[9]

By control and domination, then, we believe we can eliminate uncertainty and all risk.

So, in the political field we see the domination compulsion in the passion for the control of technology and automation and in the arms and space races. The futility of the effort in the arms race, for example, can be seen in this thirty-year chart about the acquisitions by the U.S. and the U.S.S.R.:

US 1945	atomic bomb	1949 USSR
US 1948	intercontinental bomber	1955 USSR
US 1954	hydrogen bomb	1955 USSR
USSR 1957	intercontinental ballistic missile (ICBM)	1958 US
USSR 1957	unmanned satellite in orbit	1958 US
US 1960	submarine-launched ballistic missile (SLBM)	1968 USSR
US 1966	multiple warhead (MRV)	1968 USSR
USSR 1968	anti-ballistic missile (ABM)	1972 US
US 1970	multiple independently-targeted warhead (MIRV)	1975 USSR[10]

This competition continued unabated until the sudden changes within the Soviet Union and the declaration of the end of the Cold War in the nineties. Some competition remains, and the massive accumulation of nuclear warheads and weapons systems still threatens all humanity. The acquisition of nuclear weapons by Iraq was an unresolved issue in the recent Gulf War, and the trade in a wide variety of weapons continues to grow across the world as each nation or part of a nation attempts to outdistance its neighbors in military capacity.

If we can just "get ahead" far enough, we believe, we will have dominance. Then we will no longer have to worry about what may happen. The same underlying theme persists in our concepts of crime control, disaster control, and the "drug war." It also operates in the control of information attempted by U.S. officials involved in the Watergate scandal in the seventies and in the more recent Contragate affair.

Interpersonally, this domination theme shows itself in controlling others in our relationships and in family or community. We thus avoid genuine engagement with other people. We shun the risks of mistakes and failures and of conflict and rejection in interpersonal relationships. The quest for domination reinforces social roles and social rules as well. "That's the way it is" predominates in family, workplace, or community group wherever members are not allowed to question behaviors, plans, directions, relationships, or, especially, leadership. This occurs in such diverse groupings as dating couples, law firms, church parish associations, and civil rights organizations. Family "secrets" are an all too common form of control.

Within ourselves, in the personal sphere, we seek to control our mindless passions. We will eradicate any human failure or weakness by better self-control. Like weight lifting, jogging, or mind control, we need to just try harder and use more scientific techniques or technologies. Then we will master ourselves, move to the head of the class, and get promoted.

The emphasis in all three dimensions of reality is always on being in charge. Others are accountable to us, not vice-versa. We are impatient with painstaking analysis or with tentative conclusions. Neither is allowed in television news or contemporary political campaigns where the sound-bite approach to coverage and campaigns delivers only the most succinct answers to complex questions. In a wide variety of contexts, we are afraid to admit, "This is my tentative view on this...." To do so is to divulge your openness to change and that others can influence you to change. **You are weak.** The urge to domination is impatient with process, too, and with the delicate give-and-take of negotiations. This applies to arms negotiations, interpersonal bargaining, or even family or community meetings, which are often a form of negotiation. To negotiate in good faith is to give up dominance and control in the interest of some form of mutuality and interdependence.

Ultimately, we are impatient with the concept and the reality of growth within ourselves or others. Instead, the human tendency is to oversimplify, to want simple answers and problem free relationships that don't involve me having to let go of control. This becomes true in international relations and even in the intimacy of home and family.

CONSUMPTION

The dominant role we take on is that of consumers. The dominant relational mode is **consumption**, the third engine of darkness. In this worldview, there is me; and basically everything else is something I consume or use to meet my own needs. That includes other people. Dean Brackley explains:

> From the ladder model and its social pride we see how...others progressively lose their personhood and become flat and two-dimensional, so that I no longer need to do unto them as I would have them do unto me. They become means to my ends. In sexual relations, labor relations, and public policy, the others come to be treated more as objects than subjects who could make effective moral claims on me.[11]

On a socioeconomic level, we consume the earth's resources to meet our needs, without adequate thought about replenishment. In international relations, we're willing to exploit and consume the third world and its natural resources, or look upon them merely as potential purchasers of our products. Even our new-found concern for the Brazilian rain forests smacks of our self-interest as consumers. We are willing to impose on others the restraint with nature that we ourselves have not exercised with regard to our own forests or our industrial pollution. We exploit labor to make a profit, education to get ahead, and the poor and the weak when it is politically expedient. Ultimately, we even create **human debris** from the old, sick, and disabled cast-offs of our economy and lifestyle who are treated in strikingly similar ways to our discarded commodities. Similar questions can be raised about our attitudes toward our own unborn, who can be disposed of because they are inconvenient or problematic or used in fetal tissue research. John Kavanaugh writes persuasively of the "commodification of the person" where marketing and consuming ultimately reveal us to ourselves as things and we treat others and ourselves in that context.[12]

At the community and interpersonal level, we exploit and consume our friends and relationships, without adequate concern for their wants and needs. We think that we can buy friendship and love by doing and paying, without risking the involvement in other people's lives. We want to be able to go home to family or community and have them meet our needs for relaxation, food, companionship, or privacy, but without cost to ourselves. In Jesuit communities, for example, this is captured in the image of community as men's club and the almost visceral resistance to smaller, intentional community that makes demands upon each member to be more than a consumer of goods and services.

In the personal arena, we are what we possess, and the inner dynamic of what we have drives us to want to own more and more.

> People are first tempted to solve insecurity by having or consuming things. This is the most immediate and "acceptable" of the paths promising security. Individualism and covetousness strengthen each other. Depending little on God and detached from the neighbor, the individualist readily seeks security in things. This reinforces both that reluctance to share which fosters hunger and homelessness and the social alienation that blocks collective efforts to solve common problems.[13]

In the ultimate consumerism, we even treat ourselves as commodities. Our skills, health, intelligence, education, and body are things to be consumed, used up, and not nurtured or replenished. People in social ministry or social change work can be among the worst offenders in this regard, burning themselves out physically as well as emotionally, psychologically, and spiritually—all for the most noble of causes. With this attitude comes a kind of self-loathing which manifests itself especially in the compulsiveness of overeating or excessive drinking, or in buying binges. It is the betrayal of the logic of creation where, instead of seeing ourselves as co-creators with God, we humans are radically devalued and things become invested with inflated worth, power, and even sanctity. Kavanaugh writes in terms of the "personification of the commodity" where things are cloaked in personal characteristics and can substitute for personal relationships.[14]

ISOLATION

As a result, or as a cause, we draw into ourselves in **isolation**, our fourth engine of darkness. We withdraw in uncaring ways and intolerance of other people, in personal and political survivalism, and in the loss of communality in church, community, town and village, and nation. It is a radical denial of our common humanity and a rejection of the primordial communality of the original vision of Yahweh in the Genesis stories.

In its socioeconomic manifestations, our politics took on the we-they of U.S. foreign policy that was so sadly manifest for much of the eighties in the frequently isolated U.S. votes in the United Nations. In the 1992 presidential primary campaigns this same attitude spilled over into this decade in the new isolationism of "America first" politics. At home, there was the political mean-spiritedness of the eighties embodied in what Administration Budget Director David Stockman called the "pigs at the trough" economic politics of the 1981 budget. It was accompanied by widespread disregard for the poor, "blaming the victim" in rapes and domestic violence, fraternity celebrations at executions around the country, and, in Georgia where I was at the time, the call for hangings in county squares. We have engaged in a national "move to suburbia" that can be actual or psychological, a commute to the suburban ring or withdrawal into an air-conditioned, TV-or-stereo-buffered womb or tomb. We have chosen what Robert Bellah calls our "lifestyle enclaves" and effectively blinded ourselves to the growing number and severity of economic, social, political, and cultural problems.

Even our social issues tend to become isolated in the heyday of single-issue politics. For some, the wrenching of domestic programs on the Reagan economic rack alienated those who fed the hungry from those who clothed the naked. For others, the urgency of their own concerns or inconsistency of their positions have separated people working on peace from those striving to end abortions. Whatever the causes, the connectedness that Martin Luther King brought to civil rights and opposition to the Vietnam War is a rare commodity in the political marketplace.

At the interpersonal and communal level, our isolationism shows up in an unwillingness to invest in community, in a withdrawal from the people with whom we live. We are too tired to play with the kids, attend a parent-teacher meeting tonight, or listen to our spouse's day. As John Kavanaugh put it in these board dialogues, we have established our own "demilitarized zones and non-aggression pacts" in our families and religious communities. We say to one another in effect, "If you don't talk about my problem with overeating, I won't talk about your problem with late night TV."

Donna Markham speaks of religious communities as "a metaphor for the larger global community,"[15] where the concepts of disarmament and interdependence both have a role. Her analysis, important in its own right and connecting the individual-communal-systemic, can be useful for families and other groups as well. Because of underlying fear, Markham explains, many members of religious communities "engage in behaviors that distance us from, protect us from, and cause us to threaten one another in much the same way that fear causes the superpowers to engage in their neurotic and potentially suicidal behavior."[16] The fear is rooted in significant feelings of personal and corporate inadequacy, fueled by ambiguity, role insecurity, powerlessness, and loss of status in a radically changing church and world. Religious members then can be tempted to arm themselves against "impending crises of diminishment and the death of what once was." They may live in "peaceful coexistence," but all the while they are cleverly armed against intrusion. Images of "Cold War," "retaliation," and "furthering the arms race" all may be appropriate in such a situation, Markham says, to describe a community's passive-aggressive behaviors, privatized lifestyles, repression, avoidance, withdrawal, and anger manifested in caustic criticism and worse. Self-destruction of the community may well result.

Members of such communities must be "disarmed by one another for the mission, as Jesus disarmed people by forgiveness, compassion, and reconciliation."[17] The openness that can replace our defensiveness must include addressing one another on the affective level "about our fears, our hopes, and our joys...." We must rediscover and renew our sense of self-acceptance and belief in our own and one another's basic goodness, since our defensiveness is often rooted there. We must put aside "our need to be self-protected, highly defended" and the ways we have become "extremely self-sufficient and self-reliant to the exclusion of one another."

Although we may not engage in such self-sufficient behavior intentionally, and although such overly developed self-reliance may result from a need to protect ourselves, we are essentially trying to keep ourselves safe from each other. We harbor the myth that our own private experiences and struggles are unique and unable to be understood or tolerated by others. Such a lack of interdependence results in suspiciousness and anxiety that can only reinforce our isolation. By interpreting the metaphor, we can see that the challenge we face today is whether we will respond to one another in a manner radically divergent from our current national stance. Will we witness to the possibility of a world based on openness, mutual respect, and healthy interdependence, or rather, will we in our communities continue to live defended, privatized lives alerted and prepared for ultimate destruction and death? Or will we provoke a new charge of meaning and life through our communal witness, a charge that will spark intensified commitment to Jesus' mission of justice and peace?[18]

Only then can we engage more effectively in mission together, especially the mission of building the reign of God.

When isolationism is in full control at the communal level, we rule out healthy confrontation, even when dealing with conflict is a necessary step toward becoming a true faith community. "Conflict is necessary—without it the group will not grow."[19] We do our own thing, and defy others to make claims upon us. We become intolerant of pluralism in our church parish, workplace, or family or community. The game is avoidance, and the most poignant new image of it is the escalating use of personal earphones by people riding in the same automobile or walking on the street together.

On a personal level, isolationism means unwillingness to risk opening ourselves to God or to any other person. At best, we have an extremely private Jesus-and-me spirituality. "Nobody understands," we say to ourselves. My experience of joy, sorrow, achievement, or failure is unique to me. "I'll take care of myself," we say, because no one else cares or could understand what I am going through. As the song said, "I am a rock, an island."

MYTHS, ESPECIALLY INVULNERABILITY

Beneath all of this darkness, there lay the world of **myths**, discussed earlier in chapter two. These fundamental life themes created and upheld much of the framework of our experiences of darkness. They are fed by the other engines of darkness, and legitimize them in turn. Principal among these, but by no means the only one, is the **myth of invulnerability**. We ourselves, individually, as a nation, and in certain select groupings, are invulnerable to harm, impervious to weakness, standing above the flow of human frailty. We are invulnerable or we aspire to be.

Powerful myths of manifest destiny and national invulnerability operate on the national level. We are the good guys; we wear the white hats; our cause is always just. John Wayne and others like him win all the wars on the silver screen, whether against hostile Indians, warring Germans and Japanese, rebellious confederates, or the Vietcong. The hero is invulnerable and violent. As Deborah Prothrow-Stith comments:

> The superhero is always successful, always rewarded, never hurt badly, and is always on hand for the sequel. The superhero invariably chooses a violent way to solve problems, considers violence fun, has no guilt, and really enjoys being violent.[20]

The superhero's violence is also an extreme form of the competition and domination engines discussed earlier.

Similarly, hard work definitely equals success, the myths tell us. Therefore, except for a few of those whom Ronald Reagan dubbed "the truly needy," the poor really are lazy and no good. And, if we are the good and honorable nation, then evil, in even mythic proportions, is always outside of ourselves. President Reagan, a grand myth-maker and story-teller, articulated what had long been the accepted myth with his tag on the USSR as "the evil empire." We, by implication, embodied goodness in the world.

On the family or community level, the invulnerability myth forbids ever admitting weakness in or to the group. From our school days to our adult jobs, we answer "O.K." to the question, "How did it go today?" We actually had a terrible day, but we are not going to let on how we really screwed it up or how others hurt us. We cover up the fact that pain and failure are part of all our individual journeys, and sharing that hurt is one of the chief ways of easing and understanding it. Sharing the hurt lies at the heart of intimacy, the flip-side of invulnerability. Hammett and Sofield describe the stress of intimacy:

> We have an urge to share our true feelings, but we fear that by doing so we will make ourselves vulnerable and will be rejected or criticized. The questions for each person are: Can I trust these people? How far can I trust them? Do I really want to trust them? Will they keep my confidence? Is it worth the investment of myself that intimacy requires?
>
> Intimacy is probably the most stressful of all human experiences. It reveals a capacity to share with others our deepest joys, aspirations, anxieties, and problems. In an intimate relationship we are called to step out from behind our facades and expose ourselves in the nakedness of our limitations, weaknesses, and poverties....
>
> To do this requires a great deal of love and trust—not only expressed by the other person but also by ourselves. The risk and vulnerability entailed can only be sustained if we are self-accepting....The ability to risk this openness presumes that we have had other persons in our lives with whom we had intimate relationships. Through their affirmation we have learned to be comfortable while being open and trusting.[21]

This intimacy and vulnerability are part of the relationships of any healthy family or faith community.

Pain and failure are also part of any group's life. In families and religious communities, however, we mimic the denial of individuals. Maintaining the appearance of having it all together, the invulnerabili-

ty myth at work, we say to the world and to one another, "Our marriage is wonderful" or "Oh, our community's fine." This denial, for
example, is in widespread use today by many religious congregations
with clearly terminal demographics. Underneath the "we're O.K."
facade, there's something dreadfully wrong; but we are not going to
let on. We will not admit that part of any group's life process involves
some dying, letting go and beginning again. We will not let ourselves
honestly disagree, argue, or learn from our mistakes. Choosing to pre-
tend and not face the dying, we cannot evaluate and reshape how we
might live together into the future. By not facing failure and pruning
away the dead or destructive aspects of our relationships, we often
doom the entire group, marriage, or community. So strong is the
denial that we still will not acknowledge it long after the corpse is
buried.

Another way that invulnerability operates at the group or communal
level is in the denial of the termination of any group itself. Termination
occurs whenever any members move or are transferred, the task of
a work group is completed, a class graduates, a child leaves home to
get married, or death occurs. Many groups are notoriously bad at
admitting their own vulnerability: they will not always live together,
work together, and enjoy life together. Termination, however, is
extremely stressful, and so is denied, as if the group will live forever.[22]
Some pastors exemplify this pattern when they exit their parish shortly after the announcement of personnel changes, without giving themselves or their parish the opportunity to grieve. In doing so, they often
hinder their own ability to invest in a new parish community. They
also hamper the parish community's ability to welcome a new pastor.
But too many priests seem to think that the celebrating and grieving
of leave-taking are inappropriate for them. They cannot cry. They are
invulnerable.

Personally, we play at invulnerability whenever we do not acknowledge our own need for the group, for sharing, or for intimacy. We
deny the loneliness and even anguish which is part of the human condition, no matter how close the group or how good the marriage.[23]
Versions of the self-made man often embodied the myth at this personal level. Versions of the liberated woman who could be perfect
professional, perfect wife, and super-mom have been added to the
myth's credits. Our national obsession with health, diet, and exercise
is one way of denying aging and even death. Our high-tech medical
establishment can cure whatever ails us. People of faith pray for others in need, never for themselves. We are never angry or frustrated

with God. We never acknowledge personal sin or failure. Evil is always outside of myself: in my family members, in my coworkers, in my community, or in the government or church leaders. Left to my own resources, I can make it alone. **I can do it.**

If I do admit personal problems to myself, the response is a bootstrap spirituality in which I myself will fix this. If there is something the matter with my behavior in my family or community, I can take care of it. If my prayer is a wasteland of dryness, it is because I have not tried hard enough. If I do not seem to be handling food, alcohol, or overwork very well, I just need to buckle down and try harder. *I* **can do it.**

The Triadic Insight

It is often only through our experiences of darkness that we come to new light, to new insights. So it was for the National Board of Social Ministries in facing competition, domination, consumption, isolation, and myths, especially invulnerability, and their influence in society, in groups, and in ourselves. In considering these five engines of darkness, initially we were not certain of the causal interrelationships. Was one primary? The economic system's impact, some argued, was critically important for all three levels of reality. That thesis alone, we realized, could not support the dark weight of all we had seen. Some participants suggested that our reflection should underscore human greed and sinfulness in the personal sphere; there we would find the underlying and first cause.[24] That too, however, did not seem justifiable. Explanations that singled out sin or a lack of basic experiences of being loved also failed the test. So, too, would reliance on Bellah's individualism as a sole cause. What then was the one underlying explanation?

Even as we tried to answer that question, we came to realize that the task which we had set ourselves, of isolating the one key factor, was itself part of the problem. Blaming single forces in one of the three spheres was itself a source of darkness. Even more, concentrating our efforts to create a better world on only one of the three sectors seemed to us to invite a negative result. Three examples were offered to illustrate that point. We all knew of experiences of oppressive reformers in movements for social or economic justice who had exploited their own friends and followers and whose revolutions became new dictatorships. We also recognized what we called "the

quiche and wine crowd" of community life reformers in religious congregations. They were those whose in-groups concealed a kind of
effete narcissism divorced from social reality or personal struggle.
Similar insularity could be found among prayer groups or singles
groups in some parishes whose interest focused on the group without
regard for the wider world outside. They were a form, perhaps, of
what Bellah and his coauthors would later call "lifestyle enclaves."
And, lastly, we were well aware of the navel-gazing of a false introspec-
tion which was unengaged with either social reality or a concrete
human community.[25]

The entry into light and hope, then, was to be found in the insight
that the individual, communal, and systemic dimensions of reality
were dialectic or interpenetrating. Because the same engines of darkness were operative in all three sectors, addressing them in only one
or two was deceptive and even self-defeating. Group participant
Albert Thelen put it this way:

> Those three levels so interpenetrate each other that it's impossible to do
> anything effective or adequate or complete, whether social analysis or
> dealing with social reality, if we don't take into account all three dimen-
> sions. Even if you're dealing with two of them and ignoring one, you're
> in trouble in terms of getting anything done holistically.[26]

Our own personal darkness is tied to that of the world and of others
with whom we live and work. The world's darkness is mimicked in our
own hearts. And those around us, especially our enemies, are driven
by the same forces of evil that tempt us.

The antidote to the darkness of injustice, then, lies not just in the
efforts we exert in the socioeconomic sphere. It depends equally as
well on building effective families and communities and deepening
our own spiritual lives. Our response must be multifaceted, three
dimensional, **triadic**, because the same engines of darkness are operative in all three dimensions and reinforce one another across the sectors. We called this "the triadic insight," or "the triad." Sounding a bit
like a computer part, the triad represents the integral nature of both
the evil we confront in darkness and the quality of light that dispels it.
The diagram below tries, however imperfectly, to get at the unity and
interpenetration of the three dimensions.

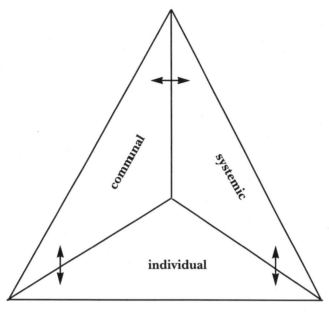

THE TRIAD

For pursuers of **faithjustice**, since we often are already engaged in the struggle in the public sphere, it seems important to underscore the critical role of the communal and the individual levels. It is there that we are most likely to be negligent and even destructive. When we act in this way, we reinforce the very powers of darkness against which we struggle in our work for justice and peace. That is the triadic insight. Roger Haight adds to this insight a practical reason focused on the well-being of the person confronting social injustices:

> We saw how precisely the social sin that dominates today's complex world threatens to crush human beings not only materially by its concrete effects but also spiritually. It saps the energy out of human freedom itself. The way to resist this sin, after therapy, lies in the effort to attack and change the very structures that cause the damage. Moreover, this has to be done corporately, through group behavior, or the individual will scarcely survive the discouragement of constant defeat. Individuals alone cannot resist institutional sin. We must function as groups which themselves become public institutions of grace.[27]

Justice-seekers then will find entry into the triad's light side at the point of building communities. These are not communities focused primarily on their own needs, but those concerned for **faithjustice**. Such an effort involves community "with its face towards the world," as Joseph Daoust put it, honestly looking at the social reality around it while simultaneously attentive to the individual journeys of its members and the quality of their life together.

This community level will not be the point of entry into the triad of individual-communal-systemic light for all believing people, certainly not for those whose proclivity is to see faith as a matter of personal or community concern and to divorce the systemic realities. For them, the systemic or social justice level will be the point of access. There is a unity here of all three dimensions, reflecting an awareness of the operation of forces of both darkness and light. All three dimensions actually have to be kept in focus because of their interpenetration. To achieve that balance for justice-seekers, attention must be placed on building **faithjustice** communities. For others, the attention must be placed on the social and systemic. As John Kavanaugh put it,

> ...those people who think we've got to change community or say we've got to pray more must come to realize that we can't even pray without this social dimension. We can't have community without it.[28]

Failure on their part to attend to the systemic will allow the powers of darkness operating freely at the systemic level to invade and reinforce the darkness in the communitarian and personal levels.

This triadic insight was not born out of the sterile logic of some isolated group analysis and reflection. In fact, in the two-year process in which we had been engaged, the social ministry board had visited a number of communities of light and hope engaged in the common task of building a better society, even in the face of overwhelming odds. In the peace movement in Seattle were small communities such as the Ground Zero community of Jim and Shelley Douglass. They were not only passionately engaged in the struggle against war and militarism, but living simple and prayerful lives together. In the South Bronx small groups of religious people worked one building at a time in reclaiming a neighborhood community from the economic and social devastation. Their Palm Sunday procession through the very midst of the destruction was a prayerful embodiment of the rebirth of new life. Religious engaged in Native American ministry, though separated by thousands of miles, had created a letter-writing network among themselves to share their struggles and to exchange insights into their ministry.

Finally, groups like the Jesuit Volunteer Corps, with whom many of us worked, had explicitly named community and personal interiority as goals on a par with, and intrinsic to, their commitment to social justice.

For so many of these different groups across the country, fidelity to one another and to prayer was a source of light and hope in the midst of the struggle for a more just society. Accepting the evil and vulnerability in themselves, made easier in the context of a supportive community, was part of being able to do justice and even to live in community with one another. John Kavanaugh summarizes this integration as follows:

> In the process of sharing and deepening a living corporate faith, a community will recognize that if it is not possible for a group of mutually committed persons to struggle honestly with their **own** propensities to injustice, competition, non-responsibility, they will hardly be justified in challenging those same patterns in the society at large which they criticize....If they are able to face and purify the patterns of injustice in their lives together, they will be able to bring greater compassion as well as insight to those patterns which are found at broader social and political levels.[29]

This kind of triadic insight also helps activists to see the connection among the issues in which they were involved, to know that inadequate and even punitive welfare programs, for example, are a part of a larger fabric of society into which is woven the arms race, inadequate housing, teen pregnancy, and racial and ethnic discrimination. In the darkness, social service and social justice can be isolated from one another; one issue can be separated from another. In the light, the connections are plain for those who can see.

At the end of this two year odyssey, our group developed a more formal statement of the triadic insight tailored to the realities of Jesuit life and communities. Initially, the statement disclaimed the search for primary causes in trying to understand social injustice and its impact in our personal lives and among social groups. Instead, it underscored the interpenetration of the three dimensions of reality. Adequate analysis could not be done by concentrating on, or even beginning with, only one of the three. The three realms are so interrelated that their "causality is mutual, and so it is ineffectual to focus on only one dimension." The results of focusing on only one dimension were then described:

- If an individual or a religious congregation focuses on just personal well-being and development, without attending to problems of family or community life and unjust social structures, that effort is merely therapeutic, **ad hoc**.

- If we focus only on social structures, without a complementary emphasis upon the interior life of prayer and upon communalism, there is no long-range interior conversion or sustaining power (e.g. burnout in an individual).
- If family relationships and community are in focus to the exclusion of personal prayer and social reality, it leads to survivalism, self-gratification, and group maintenance without a group-transcending commitment or goal.

The underlying triadic insight was affirmed on the positive side by "an inspection of the working of God's grace." God was seen as entering our lives holistically. Authentic interior and individual change, wrought by grace, necessarily must lead to changes in community relationships and one's stance before social structures. Conversion involves a whole new way of life.[30]

At the heart of this conversion was "the acceptance of our vulnerability as creatures wherein we are related to God and others, not in terms of domination and control, but in terms of invitation and the risks of faith, hope, and love." Economic, political, personal, and interpersonal domination invert this relationship, occurring systematically in all three sectors of reality. Thus they must be addressed in all three, the positive results of which were described as follows:

> When the three realms are united, as for example in prayerful and socially conscious community, we experience a strong bondedness and moments of real light. Community is then seen not just as a satisfaction of my personal need, but as a generative and apostolic force for good. Community life also serves, then, to test our own lives of prayer as well as the members' commitment to social justice. When community is lived **truthfully**, this happens by its very nature—we MUST be both prayerful and socially conscious! Then it also can serve as the starting point for our efforts to address the realities of social injustice.

As a group of social ministers, we then concluded that social analysis and action for structural change cannot be authentic without a commitment to community and interiority. Similarly, any effort at changing communities cannot succeed without the dimensions of interiority and commitment to justice. And any growth in prayer demands the commitment to justice in the world and to community.

This two-year process and its conclusions actually accomplished two purposes. It deepened my own insights and reflections into the nature of social injustice and its moving forces, the engines of darkness. The process also awakened an awareness of the profound connections between social justice and injustice and the ways we live, work, and pray as communities, families, and individuals. This second conclusion, with its emphasis on the communal dimension for those in social ministry, was most unexpected, but really should not have been for a number of reasons.

In the first place, this insight into the importance of building communities that face the world, **faithjustice** communities, is actually in keeping with the action of Yahweh in history:

> The same God who came to the aid of an oppressed people and formed them into a covenant community continues to hear the cries of the oppressed and to create communities which are responsive to God's word.[31]

This is the same direction taken by Jesus, who, critical of his own social system, "begins to form a community which will shape society in radically alternative ways."[32] This direction is followed in our own time in the renewed interest in various small Christian prayer and action groups, most especially the base Christian communities of the third world which are clearly facing outward.

Secondly, the very process itself confirmed the importance of the communal level to those seeking a more just society. Our experience as participants was that moving through social analysis and theological reflection as a group brought us to insights and conclusions beyond any one of us working alone or simply the compilation of individual insights. There is an energy and power in community that helps us to move beyond our ordinary boundaries and see more deeply and widely into both social reality and its intersection with the communal and personal. In effect our own "entry" into the triad at the level of the community which we had formed over several years gave us that power. Even the modes of cooperation, service, vulnerability, and simplicity, which were part of our community's way of proceeding, directly contrasted with the modes of darkness seen as operative in all dimensions of the triad, namely isolation, domination, invulnerability, and consumption.[33] That mode of proceeding may also have enabled us to see them more clearly for what they were.

Thirdly, the process supported the effectiveness of the Pastoral Circle, while underlining certain process aspects, including the community involvement. Our particular community was enriched by diversity in temperament, region, academic training, and work experiences, though not diverse in religion, race, gender, or nationality. We had also engaged in insertion among the poor to broaden our experience, prayed together, shared our hopes, fears, and vulnerability, and provided simple services to one another in preparation for this endeavor. All this increased the level of trust and heightened the desire to work together on common goals. Professor Robert Michael Franklin comments that, from a similar experience of his students who shared deep experiences of social realities with one another, "a profound spiritual bond emerges which resembles a covenant relationship."[34] This reiterates the importance of doing the Pastoral Circle process in a diverse group and the strength which can be found there if community building is factored into the ongoing process.

Finally, the developments sketched out in this chapter improve our insights into **faithjustice**. They expand the traditional approach of many social activists from the dyad of persons and social structures into a more complex and helpful triad of individuals, communities, and social structures. The triadic insight also enriches the connection between religious faith and social justice, helping us to see how traditional personal and community faith dimensions and practices repeat the patterns of, and are related to, social and systemic realities. This can help spiritual directors, pastoral counselors, educators and others better understand the relevance of social reality for even the most personal pastoral ministry.

The triad also strengthens our ability to assess the reality of justice and injustice in which we live and move using three vantage points instead of two. Thus, it expands the frontiers on which we must act in pursuit of a world transformed by **faithjustice**. Chapter four will explore a wide range of implications for living out this commitment, rooted in our better understanding of the contours of darkness and light. By coming to understand the triadic darkness that underpins injustice, we have also come to see that the path by which we can walk in the light has personal, communal, and systemic dimensions.

CHAPTER FOUR

Walking in the Light

I believe that unarmed truth and unconditional love will have the final word in reality. That is why right temporarily defeated is stronger than evil triumphant.

MARIN LUTHER KING, JR.
NOBEL ACCEPTANCE SPEECH
DECEMBER 10, 1964

On the two sides of the rotunda of the State Capitol in Atlanta, outside the third floor entrances to the House and Senate chambers, a symbolic division of forces occurred. On one side, near the Speaker's office, were those–predominantly male, white, and middle-aged or older–representing society's big interests: the banks, industries, large farms, insurance companies, bar associations, doctors, nursing homes, and such. On the other side were those–as likely to be female, black, or young–representing consumers, tenants, elders, nurses, persons with disabilities, and poor families. Official and unofficial lobbyists on the first side generally were well-paid, with significant budgets for entertainment and expenses. They were considered to have clout. "What could we hope to do for our clients," I asked, "without such resources?" The experienced lawyer I worked with responded, "Our primary resources are our expertise in the areas of our clients' concerns, our persistence, and extremely hard work. Good legislators will be influenced by those far more than fancy parties or anything else."

* * *

When I resigned legal services in Baton Rouge in the spring of 1984, I grieved for months. I had been associated with legal services, primarily in Atlanta's well-respected program, since my first law school summer in 1970. I had "grown up" in the world of legal services for the poor, both before and after my ordination. The leaving decision, then, was wrapped in a sense of deep personal failure and the shattering of youthful dreams. The causes of my

99

leaving only aggravated the pain. There were acute racial tensions on the agency board, a racially motivated refusal to review the performance of the agency director, and the devastating effect of such leadership upon legal representation for poor clients. I had come to realize, though, that even as managing attorney of the downtown office I could do little to effect real change unless agency management and the fratricidal board of directors were both replaced. That, as history proved, would not happen. The program's travails continued for years.

* * *

In the late eighties, in Paraguay, Father Don Bahlinger had had enough. Pastor of the parish of San Ignatio in the town bearing the same name, Don had repeatedly protested to the government about the lack of health services for the people. The government of President Stroessner had constructed a modern brick hospital in the town as proof of the long-term dictator's compassion. The problem was that they just never put it into service. A new government still had done nothing.

After consultation with his spiritual director, Father Bahlinger decided that his annual retreat should be transformed into a period of prayer and fasting–in the waiting room area–until the hospital should be opened. He had hardly been there a day when two hundred of the people from the surrounding area showed up for a Mass at the hospital. Several days later, hundreds of campesinos, a number of priests, the local bishop, and the local and national media were gathered around the hospital and Don's prayerful fast and vigil.

Suddenly, scarcely five days after he had begun his personal witness for justice, government trucks arrived with equipment for the hospital. After the equipment was unloaded, the townspeople scoured the facility clean. Then, the hospital opened to serve the needs of the entire area. It was a tale Don told me with true delight as we toured the hospital and met some of the staff and patients a year later. I treasured the story, an all too infrequent victory in the struggle against institutional injustice. It was as if one person's persistence had become a gift of life to an entire region.

* * *

Two of our Washington, D.C. community returned tired, but elated, from a weekend retreat of women and men active in Central American advocacy. The retreat had been an experience of mutual support and encouragement, and it provided renewed resolve for the future. Among the many experiences they described, one comment stood out. After discussions in small groups, an older veteran of the struggle for justice and peace in Central America stood up. She concluded her remarks on perseverance against almost overwhelming forces with these simple words of hope: "The seed does not know the flower."

This chapter brings us a full turn on the Pastoral Circle to talk of planning and action. We have sampled the analysis component in chapters one, two, and three, and done some theological reflection across all three chapters. Now we ask ourselves what sustains us and the veterans and survivors around us in social ministry for the long haul? What are the ways of life amid so much death in all three sectors of human life and society? Where does God's spirit move, and how does our God nourish, inspire, and energize us in the service of justice and peace? I would suggest that we return to the concluding insights of the last chapter. There we can find the means for us to continue to construct the reign of God in the face of injustice, violence, and death in our own country and across the world.

The lesson of chapter three is that hopefulness in the face of injustice is rooted in the individual, communal, and systemic sectors of reality. Our analysis revealed that to serve justice we must concentrate simultaneously on individual conversion, group and community commitment, and systemic action. Activist Patricia Natali explains, using imagery of the prophet Micah:

> Micah 6:8 exemplifies this integration by instructing us to act justly, love tenderly and walk humbly with our God. Regardless of where we start real progress on the human journey includes the other two as well. It is not possible to "act justly" unless we love tenderly. Without love justice is cold and harsh and can be the vehicle of fresh injustices. And we are empowered to act justly and love tenderly by walking humbly with our God, a God of love and justice. If we begin with "love tenderly" justice must be included or it is just sentimental and naive. How can one love victims of injustice suffering economic deprivation if we are not, at the same time, working to create economic structures which remove the exploitation. If we begin with "walk humbly with God" we are not removed from the world, but engaged where God is, in the midst of the events of the world. This God with whom we walk humbly is the God of justice who empowers us to act justly and the God of love who desires us to love tenderly. From this perspective, the separation between spirituality and justice is difficult to see.[1]

Reflecting on this popular quotation reminds us of the triadic unity: the systemic in "acting justly," the communal in "loving tenderly," and the individual in "walking humbly with our God.

Put another way, our pilgrimage involves finding our way along three separate, but connected, paths. To act justly, we must be able to walk along the path of justice that involves our personal lifestyles, avoids deep and dangerous pitfalls, and leads us to radical ways of working and living. To love tenderly, we must find our way down a path of love with a community of sisters and brothers committed to the same journey. And to walk humbly with God, we must travel a path of reverence enlightened by prayer and a renewed sense of Sabbath.

The Path of Justice

Perhaps surprisingly, the path to a more just world begins with our own personal lifestyles. It is as if this were the narrow path spoken of by Jesus, and we cannot travel it weighed down with too much baggage. Jim Hug comments in his study of faith communities committed to social action that, "Most of the groups interviewed for this study showed some attraction to a poorer life-style and greater identification with the poor as a way to live Gospel values and free themselves for more responsive and discerning Christian love."[2] He also acknowledges that, "It is in part a testimony to the subtle power of economic factors that by their own admission so few have been able to follow that attraction." Despite the difficulty, the almost instinctual attraction to simplicity of lifestyle among those committed to social action confirms its importance for all of us.

Simplicity of lifestyle takes many forms.[3] Such "lifestyle connections" in pursuit of active solidarity with the poor are, in Jim McGinnis' words, "as unlimited as our imaginations."[4] McGinnis names a few for our consideration: (1) a "world bank" on the dinner table to remind the family to eat sacrificially and to share the savings with the world's hungry; (2) using public transportation as an experience of the inconvenience with which the poor live daily; (3) "eating connectedly" that links consumer decisions to farmworker questions and other corporate practices; (4) sharing one's clothes with those in need; and (5) an "exchange system" for purchases that circulates an item out of the house for every one brought in. Thomas Clancy provided two other rules of thumb worth noting: (1) if you haven't worn it in a year—four seasons—give it away; and (2) if you haven't read it in thirty days or used it as a reference, give it to a library. The latter suggestion is probably a tougher one for those of us whose homes and offices are spilling over with books. The environmental movement can provide many other examples, just from the point of view of ecological responsibility.

McGinnis also reminds us that poverty is an evil, and that our goal is not to play at being poor. Rather, we are challenged, first, to let go of the privileges we have **at the expense of the poor**.[5] Here we might think of U.S. consumption of so much of the world's goods or energy. Or we might consider how profit margins are widened too often at the expense of underpaid workers or at cost to low-income consumers. Or we might analyze the connection between tax exemptions and deductions which some of us enjoy and their cost to the common good. Or we might connect our own comfortable personal income to the low incomes of our domestic servants or child care workers. This can usher us into a more far-reaching process of downward mobility that runs counter to the prevailing ethic of our culture. Such a move may be a real difficulty, but it can enable us to reach deeper levels within ourselves. There, following the lead of Richard Rohr, Jim Douglass, and Henri Nouwen, McGinnis says we are challenged to "let go of the need to be productive (or 'relevant'), the need to be recognized and acclaimed (or 'spectacular'), and the need to be in control (or 'powerful')."[6] Relevance, recognition, and power are our generation's versions of Christ's three temptations in the desert.

In terms of the engines of darkness, such a simple lifestyle offers a reminder to ourselves and to the world that strength does not lie in things (consumption). We need not amass possessions in order to establish ourselves as superior to others (competition and domination). Simplicity also is an affirmation of the basic truths of Genesis that God is creator, we are stewards, and the earth is for the community of humankind, not for me alone.

Dean Brackley reminds us that, while a simple lifestyle is a form of cultural resistance to compulsive consumption, "its social meaning is above all the freedom to share with those in need."[7] This would allow us to be detached materially from what we do not really need for love of Christ present to us in today's poor. This simplicity can be a form of solidarity with poor families who often have to choose between paying the rent and buying food or medicine. Such solidarity is thus possible even though our many tangible and intangible resources may prevent us from fully tasting the experience of genuine economic poverty.

Finally, the decisions we make about lifestyle as individuals, families,[8] and communities are not "playing at poverty" or "playing house." Lifestyle decisions directly enhance or undercut the work which we do in trying to make this a more just world. Either God's vision of a covenant community sharing the world's gifts is brought to fruition in the way each of us lives, or we spin off into me-first lifestyle enclaves that require high walls and guards to fend off the world's hungry. Lifestyle constitutes a crucial facet of living truthfully the giftedness, stewardship, and community which are at the heart of **faithjustice**. To say we have a special love for the poor and yet to live personally as if poor families were invisible puts the lie to our work for a more just and peaceful world.

The path of justice is indeed narrow. It passes between a succession of dangerous whirlpools which, like the classic Scylla and Charybdis, attempt to seduce us to destruction on one side or the other. Staying on this path involves careful attention to the means we use to achieve our ends. We cannot use power as our enemies and the enemies of the poor use power. We cannot allow anger or guilt to drive our efforts. We cannot even measure the success or failure of our work as others do.

More poetically than descriptively, what I want to say is suggested by Robert Bolt's Sir Thomas More in *A Man For All Seasons*. A heated conversation about the king's policies occurs between More and his more staunchly papist son-in-law Roper:

MORE. ...The law, Roper, the law. I know what's legal not what's right. And I'll stick to what's legal.

ROPER. Then you set man's law above God's!

MORE. No, far below; but let me draw your attention to a fact—I'm not God. The currents and eddies of right and wrong, which you find such plain sailing, I can't navigate. I'm no voyager. But in the thickets of the law, oh, there I'm a forester. I doubt if there's a man alive who could follow me there, thank God...

ROPER. So now you'd give the Devil benefit of law!

MORE. Yes. What would you do? Cut a great road through the law to get after the Devil?

ROPER. I'd cut down every law in England to do that!

MORE. Oh? And when the last law was down, and the Devil turned round on you—where would you hide, Roper, the laws all being flat? This country's planted thick with laws from coast to coast—man's laws, not God's—and if you cut them down—and you're just the man to do it— d'you really think you could stand upright in the winds that would blow then? Yes, I'd give the Devil benefit of law, for my own safety's sake.[9]

For me, the conversation stretches between the absolute idealism of Roper, saying we do this-or-that because our cause is right and all else be damned, and More the almost-pragmatic realist. If he was a real pragmatist, as his conforming friends urge, More would take the king's oath and cross his fingers while doing so. But More is about means and ends. He declares that these things in the middle—these means, laws, institutions—say something about where I belong, who I am, and what matters in life. If I tear them all down, More protests, then destruction is let loose.

Put another way, we stand like Jesus before Pilate and Herod. He does not engage with either Pilate or Herod in their games, neither the power game with Pilate nor Herod's cynicism. The mob and the Jewish leaders play the power game with Pilate, but Jesus refuses although he could call up an army of angels. Then, as portrayed in that wonderful scene in the musical *Godspell*, what Herod wants from Jesus is some miracle. "Dance across my swimming pool," he taunts. He needs to see Jesus do something that will fit the scheme of how he sees the world. But Jesus just stands there in silence to Herod's utter frustration. Our response, too, if we are to avoid the darkness, often cannot be the same as those we confront. This applies to our advocacy in state legislatures or Congress, where we work without the wherewithal for substantial campaign contributions or even expense accounts. It also means that we do not use political threat or coercion as others do. We must treat our enemies with the dignity which they often deny to us and to the poor.

There is something here for all of us about means and ends, that we do not go off the path to the extremes of violence and oppressive power of our enemies. Otherwise, we become like our enemies by resort to their methods. As Martin Luther King said, "The truth will set us free." I sense in myself, for example, that I am quite capable of personal violence, especially in the face of violence against the poor. The same feelings were aroused by the 1989 killing of my Jesuit brothers in El Salvador whose only crime was to stand with the poor. But there is darkness in that reaction. Even when others engage in violence, we must "be wise as serpents," but somehow, as Jesus also said, "gentle as doves." We cannot hate as others do. Our anger must be directed, not at people, but at deeds and structures to fashion effective actions for justice.

Staying on the path of justice means that we pass between the anger generated by the injustice we see and the guilt we often experience at our own wealth, education, health, or well-being in contrast to poor people. As one psychiatrist told me in discussing the subject of burnout, guilt is often just anger turned back in on ourselves. Some people who work among the poor seem to be men and women driven primarily by anger or guilt. These are common human feelings, both anger and guilt. When they become dominant, however, we become driven to a point where we cannot see with perspective and do not take care of ourselves. We also may suffer from a form of anger-or-guilt-induced paralysis. Here we can be so immobilized by either that we can do nothing effective. Guilt then can drive us impetuously, or it can paralyze us. Both reactions are deadly traps. Neither is life-giving. Guilt can also be manipulated by others for their own purposes, as some among the poor do to meet their needs.

When we act for justice, then, it cannot be to expiate the attitudes of our parents or the fact that we may have been gifted in our own growing up. True, we may have gone to good schools, received a good education, and had good health care. Those are the benefits of creation that all people, both us and the poor, should be able to enjoy. Those gifts, however, should move us appropriately to want to share with others what we have received.

The inoculation against being driven or paralyzed or manipulated by anger or guilt is threefold. First, we must accept the limits of our own guilt in the mystery of redemption. Sure, we are all sinners, a condition shared by the rich and by the poor, as we soon learn in our ministry. But we are loved as we are, rendered lovable by God's gift of forgiveness. We then do not need to earn forgiveness or make restitution for the past good we have received in life which others may not have shared. (We may have, however, a duty in charity or justice to share our current resources.)

What then is my response to the gross inequalities which I see around me? What about the starvation in Somalia or the brutal civil war in what was Yugoslavia? What of the racism and sexism in society around me? If guilt is not the proper response, what is? Canadian theologian Gregory Baum suggests that one proper Christian response to social evil is **mourning**.[10] This is the second component of our passage between anger and guilt. We don't close our eyes to the harshness of human evil or natural disaster, but we also do not blame ourselves or others if we are not involved. We mourn. We grieve the suffering of human persons like ourselves and join our grief and mourning to that of God and of all creation. We take a moment or an hour of personal time, of our meetings, and of our prayer to attune ourselves to the suffering around us, to be one with it, and to mourn.

Then, the third response: we love freely. We move out in justice freely, because God has freed us to so love. This was the original

Genesis revelation that we are invited to be like God in loving freely—not driven by guilt or anger. We assess the needs of others, our capacity for responding in justice and love, and determine appropriate action. Walking the path of justice for any length of time means acting freely. We understand, "Yeah, I'm a sinner. I've participated in this evil of the world. I've got anger and guilt in me. But I refuse to be dominated by either." The person on the path of justice then moves forward out of love and justice, knowing that he or she is loved gratuitously and freely by God despite all this.

The path of justice then passes between two other worlds. One is the world of the powerful, marked by violence and oppression used to maintain power and privilege. Such power can be exercised even in poor communities, one poor person over another. The opposite world of the powerless is too often signaled by hopelessness, poverty, and marginalization. Our ministry for justice has to be situated somewhere in the middle of this, between and even connecting these opposing worlds.

People will say to me, "Well, I can never really be with the poor because I have resources that they don't have. I could never be completely powerless." In many ways that is true. But there is a gift that can be brought, humbly, into that environment of powerlessness and oppression, namely solidarity. It is a gift which we in social ministry must bring and from which we have much to learn. It is a graced point of encounter, part of the means that we would use to effect a more just and compassionate world. In addition there is much in the world of poor families from which we can learn. Volunteer Beth Ann Corr writes of her experience working with families with AIDS:

> Instead, I rely on the beauty and strength of my clients which lift me up just when I feel like declaring defeat.... My clients have taught me more about faith, courage and perseverance than I could have imagined. Every day they reload their slingshots and aim between the eyes of injustice, understanding that the battle will not be won swiftly or easily.[11]

This is why it is so important that we remain in touch with poor families. We also may enable the powerless to become in touch with their own power, becoming more in control of their own participation in society and their own destiny. And while we may be able to contribute in some way to this empowering, we learn some of it from them as well.

On the other side is the world of the powerful, a world to which we may have access by education, wealth, profession, friendship, or birth. When we analyze it carefully, we realize that this, too, is not a world to which we may belong, not in the fullest sense. This world of privilege is maintained by systems and structures which are fundamentally unjust, making it possible for so few to have so much and so many to live in destitution. Our stance must be one of prophecy, the ever uncomfortable role that calls people back to covenant with one another, to shared stewardship of the earth's resources, and to community. Personal friendships, available resources, the apparent possibility of doing something about world problems, and even the fatigue of the prophet may all tempt us away from the prophetic role and more deeply into the world of the privileged. It happens so easily.

To walk down the middle between these two worlds, we must act out of truth and we shall be free in that. The truth is about ourselves as sinners and graced, about both rich and poor as sinners and graced, and about God calling us to act in bridging the conflict between rich and poor. To teach the rich about the lives of the poor we need that solidarity with the poor. It enables us to ask with credibility the prophetic question about community decisions, "How does this decision being made impact the poor?" At the same time, we need to connect the poor back to the powerful. The poor sometimes will tell us this, "We don't need you working here in our community. We need you to connect us to those with resources, to the corridors of power, to the banks, to the lawmakers, to the bureaucrats." They may also tell us that we need to be working among the wealthy and powerful, that problems like racism and poverty are rooted there, not in communities of the poor and marginalized.

Somehow, this suggests that our appropriate ministry is somewhere in the center, bridging the two, while not forgoing solidarity with the poor nor prophetic challenge to the powerful. The ancient church word was *pontifex*, builder of bridges. When we get too far out on the power end, when we react in violence or oppression or force even against the oppressors, we have fallen from the path and taken the way of darkness and sin. Or when we become completely powerless, oppressed and hopeless, we can no longer minister to those around us. We cannot bring the gifts we have to the world of hopelessness and oppression. We become part of the problem, not the solution.

We must walk the path of justice, then, maintaining both solidarity with those who are poor and a prophetic voice in the world of the powerful. When that seems impossible, we might remember the thousands of Philippine citizens who peacefully placed their bodies in front of the tanks of their military in a bloodless uprising seen across the world. Their peaceful effort and the largely peaceful revolutions of Eastern Europe remind us that there is a middle ground between violent power as we have known it and the powerless submission it has forced upon people. Our task is to find and hew to that middle path.

The path of justice also passes between a third set of extremes, the darkness of failure and the seduction of success. In chapter one, I introduced the topic of failure and discussed the importance of understanding its reality in the pursuit of **faithjustice**. There and elsewhere we saw that there is a very real power of evil in our world. The truths of creation have been perverted. The **anawim** are exploited. We have forgotten their special place in God's heart, and we have become owners of creation, not stewards. In such a worldwide environment, much of what we set out to do in social justice ministry will fail. We are engaged in conflict with major forces, institutionalized injustice, systemic evil. This realization of failure, though, can be overwhelming and can drive us from this ministry.

On the other hand, if our focus is all on success—"I'm going to work on this project if it eradicates poverty or brings peace to the world"— then we are doomed to walk in darkness. If we enter into the cause of justice just for what we get out of it, that feeling of victory, then there is a problem from the outset and longevity in this work is unlikely. If we even have expectations of ongoing success for the sake of those we work with or for, the unreality of those expectations will haunt us.

To survive in this work, we have to acknowledge that we are engaged not merely in sociopolitical conflict; it is instead the way of the passion. We only get to resurrection through rejection, oppression, suffering, failure, and death. An intrinsic part of what we do in social ministry, social justice, and working with the poor is going to fail. And all of us who came into this work thinking that this would not happen to us have already, I am sure, had our eyes opened wide. Failure is now part of the fabric of our experience, woven all through this work. Shortly before his death, veteran Arkansas activist Joe Biltz wrote:

> [I]n the paradoxical words of hope spoken by the Latin American theologian, Rubem Alves, "We must live by the love of what we will never see." ...Indeed, the reality of the risk, challenge and involvement, the "costly grace," the "harsh and dreadful love," that a theology of social action demands of us, was eloquently expressed by one of the great living examples of this theology, Dom Helder Camara, when he said, "We must have no illusions, we must not be naive, if we listen to the voice of God, we make our choice, get out of ourselves and fight non-violently for a better world. We must not expect to find it easy, we shall not walk

on roses, we shall not always be aware of Divine Protection. But if we are to be pilgrims of justice and peace, we must expect the desert."[12]

Biltz introduces the theme of failure and success by speaking of "what we will never see." The prophets seldom see the fulfillment of their vision. Moses never made it to the promised land. Lincoln was assassinated before the nation was healed. Gandhi too was killed before unity and peace came to India. Pope John XXIII opened the doors and windows of the church, but never even saw the work of the Second Vatican Council completed. Martin Luther King, Jr., died in Memphis in the midst of the civil rights struggle. Oscar Romero was murdered before peace could begin in El Salvador. Sometimes it is only the deaths of the prophets that bring people to their senses, or that convince the people that they themselves must become prophetic.

In talking of what we will not see, Biltz also reminds us of one Marxist critique of religion. They argued that religion was the "opiate of the people" because, in view of the promise of life hereafter, religious people, including the poor themselves, would tolerate hell on earth. In one sense Marx was correct in that we do not anticipate the fullness of the reign of God within the present confines of history. The reign is never complete, always becoming. Justice is never fully enfleshed in our world's structures. The poor will always be with us...to some degree. But, on the other hand, Marx could not have been more wrong. The gospels teach clearly that Christians must not tolerate injustice. They will be judged, as Jesus taught in the 25th chapter of Matthew, on their response to the poor in their midst.

Even more powerfully, though, the Christian mystery, sealed in the life of Jesus, contains within itself a dynamic that charges us to do what we are called to do **regardless of successful results**. The operative word is **fidelity**. Thomas Merton comments in the context of peacemaking:

> And then this: do not depend on the hope of results. When you are doing the sort of work you have taken on, essentially an apostolic work, you may have to face the fact that your work will be apparently worthless and even achieve no result at all, if not perhaps results opposite to what you expect. As you get used to this idea you start more and more to concentrate not on the results but on the value, the rightness, the truth of the work itself.[13]

We follow this Jesus who went ahead and lived in fidelity to the Father and to the reign of God, to that dual passion of his, regardless of results! **This awareness can make us the most dangerous of fanatics, the most subversive of subversives, the most unbending of radicals.**

We follow the one who lived in the full awareness of the truth of who he was created to be and how we were to live as God's covenanted people. Nothing else mattered to him. He went to his death apparently having failed to convince his people and their leaders of the need for conversion to this gospel. It was only after his death that his way was vindicated. As his disciples, then, it should not matter to us whether we succeed or fail. We, like Christ, must live in fidelity to the call to be God's people with that special care for the **anawim**. We must live that way, successful or not, because we leave it in the hands of God to bring the reign to fulfillment in God's own time. We, in fact, should be those who are least concerned about results, least dismayed by failure, and least dependent upon success as the criteria for continuing our commitment to **faithjustice**.

Writing in the context of the painful 1989 closure of the House of Affirmation in Massachusetts, Doctor Wilfred Pilette reflected on these same realities:

> Several faithful individuals had been at the center of the positive changes effected during the House's last two years. For me, they vivified Mother Teresa's famous admonition: "God does not ask us to be successful, but to be faithful." I came away from this painfully rich experience with the conviction that all quests for success are futile and should be replaced by ongoing attempts at faithfulness. This applies most obviously to our spiritual lives, in which success implies the attainment of holiness, while faithfulness admits to the continuing need for renewal. It also applies to our psychological lives, in which success promises the impossible attainment of the perfect self, while faithfulness implies a continuing struggle to become our true selves. And it applies as well to our work lives. ...One does well to heed Kipling's wise words about success and failure—to "treat those two imposters just the same."[14]

Pilette endorses ongoing attempts at faithfulness rather than futile quests for success in all aspects of life. In doing so, he runs against the dominant motivations of most reformers.

In other words, a good communist, fascist, democrat, or republican expects this or that set of results and is working to create a certain kind of society. If that does not happen, she or he is likely to be dismayed and say, "Why should I commit myself to this if it isn't working?" The changes which swept through the European Communist world may be one good example of this. But to some extent for us as Christians committed to justice it does not matter how our own efforts turn out. Our commitment to justice then should be the most powerful force for social change in the history of humanity because it is not contingent on results.

That does not mean you do dumb things! Discerning love still requires that we look for the signs of the times, analyze the world in which we live and work, assess the realities according to the gospel, and make judgments about effective action in an ongoing process. That is still necessary, still important to building the reign of God according to God's own vision. But ultimately God must bring it to fulfillment. God must raise up life from the death which we undergo in faithfully following the pattern of Jesus. We are committed to following in that pattern even though we, like Jesus before us, do not see the fulfillment of our dreams and visions. Even when we've done all of that, we will fail. And none of us likes to fail.

If failure is all there is for us, if that is our complete and over-whelming experience, however, then we may need to take action to get out of the situation we are working in. We may need to shake the dust from our feet, to commit ourselves elsewhere, to change our way of going about **faithjustice**. That is the judgment which I made in leaving legal services in Baton Rouge. This is not to suggest questioning our ultimate fidelity to working for the reign of God or total abandon-ment of the struggle for justice and peace. Rather, our decisions must be about using discerning love, analysis and reflection, to go about it differently. We walk in the middle somewhere between success and failure, each of us doing so differently in reliance upon the same Spirit that guided Jesus. We are not dependent upon results, and that rather distinguishes us from communists, capitalists, conservatives, lib-erals, whatever. Our commitment, however, is dependent upon living in the truth of acting freely with love and justice.

The best explanation for this faithful stance might be to talk of the Christian virtue of hope. Peter Henriot says, "Hope is more politically powerful than despair."[15] The late Harry Fagan named hope as the critical task of the diocesan social action office:

> The signs of the times seem to promote the "dug in" attitudes of nega-tivism, cynicism and pessimism that make us continually reach for our faith. Certainly the doubling and tripling of hot meal lines, the endless stories of once-productive, now-desperate people looking for emergency shelter and the open wounds in our society festering because of unem-ployment, drugs and violent crime cannot be easily dismissed. But the diocesan social action office that believes and acts with enough hope to

instill the confidence necessary to begin to meet, tackle and solve those problems clearly understands its role—not in a naive, idealistic sense, but in the gutsy and peaceful way of serving as a rallying point for others by symbolizing the resurrection in very concrete actions.[16]

This resort to religious language about hope is not just a psychological strategy or tactical gambit to get us through the tough tension between success and failure in the face of often overwhelming powers. It is rather to call those interested in **faithjustice** to both courage and leadership.

Courage, David Hollenbach writes, is a Christian virtue which is not just strength of will or fearlessness, but it is "strength of will **in the pursuit of justice.**"[17] Such courage takes two forms. The first is the courage of endurance of "those who suffer persecution for justice sake." The second form is one of daring, involving passion and even anger and directed towards action in the cause of justice. This courage is what cuts between success and failure, empowering us to be committed to the poor and to social change without regard to results.

Courage, however, is not enough. What is needed so badly in our society and across the world is courageous leadership. Far too many leaders actually are followers; they follow the polls, press approval, and trends. In contrast, Henri Nouwen calls for Christian leadership in words reflecting our considerations of the darkness of powerlessness, pain, and suffering:

> The task of future Christian leaders is not to make a little contribution to the solution of the pains and tribulations of their time, but to identify and announce the ways in which Jesus is leading God's people out of slavery, through the desert to a new land of freedom. Christian leaders have the arduous task of responding to personal struggles, family conflicts, national calamities, and international tensions with an articulate faith in God's real presence. They have to say "no" to every form of fatalism, defeatism, accidentalism or incidentalism which make people believe that statistics are telling us the truth. They have to say "no" to every form of despair in which human life is seen as a pure matter of good or bad luck. They have to say "no" to sentimental attempts to make people develop a spirit of resignation or stoic indifference in the face of the unavoidability of pain, suffering, and death. In short, they have to say "no" to the secular world and proclaim in unambiguous terms that the incarnation of God's Word, through whom all things came into being, has made even the smallest event of human history into Kairos, that is, an opportunity to be led deeper into the heart of Christ.[18]

The path of justice, then, must pass between extremes of anger and guilt, power and powerlessness, success and failure. It takes us along a route whose signposts are loving freely in the pattern of God, fidelity without depending on success, truth without resort to violence and oppression, and courageous leadership.

The path of justice also takes us uphill against the forces of culture and conformity that so control our society. It is a journey in resistance, as Miriam Theresa MacGillis explains:

> We must "walk the rocky hillside sowing clover"...we must. Each of us, in spite of the dark or the danger, we must pocket our seeds and go out into the night. It is where we claim the significance of our lives. In spite of everything that would reduce our power, we must sow our seeds, build our families, dignify our work, enflesh our dreams and keep our promises. We must make bread, vigils, petitions, laws, friendships, treaties, babies, dances and worship. We must believe that the darkest aspects of our humanness contain the seeds of transformation. We must resist our lack of hope, our loss of fire. We must finger our very lives and times as prayer beads, sow them on the rocky hillside.[19]

What does a lifestyle of resistance mean in this context for individuals and the communities which we found and build? Henri Nouwen speaks of resistance as "the daily life of peacemakers," not just specific acts of resistance, but our whole being resisting the powers that lead to injustice, war, and destruction. Following his lead, three aspects of this lifestyle of resistance are discussed below.

Resistance means saying "No" to the forces of death. Our most obvious "No" is to the actual use of nuclear arms, an unconscionable horror.

> It is obvious that all people who believe that God is a God of life, and especially we who proclaim that Jesus Christ came to live among us to overcome the powers of death, must say "No" to nuclear arms, a clear and unambiguous "No."[20]

But Christian resistance extends back more deeply and broadly to a "No" to the amassing of nuclear weapons because, as the Vatican has clearly stated, they kill the poor. It also requires an equally fervent "No" to the impact upon ourselves, beginning with the fears and horrors of our children. The youngest among us often see, like a king with no clothes, the horrid realities of such weapons. We are a nation which, by its amassing of nuclear arms, expresses its willingness to use them. This willingness was not only condemned by our bishops' 1983 peace pastoral, but it is a horrible judgment upon our own fears, angers, and destructiveness.

Our "No" must also extend consistently to death in all the other forms in which it parades across the face of our world. This includes abortion, the crude and exploited death of violent sports and TV shows, and the less spectacular death of our everyday lives. Consider, for example, the ways in which we objectify, judge, and dismiss (kill off) others in our conversations about them. We also talk of "writing off" others as useless individuals. We do the same with those who are aged, poor, disabled, or racial minorities. Or we think even of ourselves with self-loathing, self-rejection, and deep self-hatred reflected in, for example, our excessive consumption of alcohol, food, or drugs.

These are all ways of death, Nouwen says, because they render others or ourselves fixed, static, unchangeable, hopeless, ...dead. This is also the way much of our society thinks about people who are poor, an attitude which surely is communicated to them and absorbed by them as well. In contrast, we also may have the same attitude toward those who are rich and powerful, considering them to be beyond change. We create death whenever we judge people as incapable of change. That death takes many forms: cutting others out of our lives, giving up on ourselves ("thinking myself to death"), and even death-oriented self-indulgence in which we choose the certainty of the moment over the uncertainty of the future. Living a life of resistance, then, means saying "No"—firmly and frequently—to death in all its forms.

Resistance means saying "Yes" to life in all its forms. There is a subtle danger hidden in the anti-nuclear, anti-racism, anti-sexism, anti-abortion, anti-pollution, anti-whatever movements. A stance of perennial opposition, saying "No" to death in any of its forms, struggling constantly against death, can seduce us into becoming victims of death itself. We have all met people like this. Death in one of its forms becomes so all-consuming and gets so much of their attention and energy that it dominates their lives. They become victims of the very death which they oppose. Driven by the very forces of darkness against which they stand, their hearts are violent and warlike. They become lost to the cause of peacemaking, life, or justice which they set out to serve. A friend in Pax Christi in New Orleans described this as her experience of some others in the anti-war movement. These others, participating in a common demonstration against the Gulf War, seemed to her to be as filled with violence of language and symbols as the war they opposed. A similar example seems evident in the pro-life demonstrator who shot and killed the doctor-abortionist in Florida.

Saying "No" then is not enough to lead a life of resistance and remain on the path of justice. There must be a commensurate and even more enthusiastic "Yes" to life:

> It means that only a loving heart, a heart that continues to affirm life at all times and places, can say "no" to death without being corrupted by it. A heart that loves friends and enemies is a heart that calls forth life and lifts up life to be celebrated. It is a heart that refuses to dwell in death because it is always enchanted with the abundance of life. Indeed only in the context of this strong loving "Yes" to life can the power of death be overcome. I therefore want to say here as clearly as I can that the first and foremost task of the peacemaker is not to fight death but to call forth, affirm, and nurture the signs of life wherever they become manifest.[21]

A strong, resounding "No" is not enough; our resounding "Yes" must nurture the signs of life wherever they may be found. Violent death is big, noisy, proud, like the crowd at a political convention or in a football stadium or like the brass of a military band. Or it is quick and loud like the shots that ring out at night in a drug dominated neighborhood. Life is vulnerable, slowly growing, risking, small, hidden, soft-spoken, like all those stories of the reign of God which Jesus kept telling to the crowds and to his disciples. Life grows imperceptibly and moves graciously, which underscores the importance of serving life wherever it may be found. This would seem to underlie the work of Dan Berrigan and other peace activists in New York some years ago when they chose to visit persons in nursing homes on a regular basis.

This life-affirming approach also underscores the importance of all issue-advocates being in some ongoing person-to-person contact with poor families. Then their "No" to defense spending or poverty or hunger can be directly connected to care for specific persons—their "Yes." Saying "Yes" means finding joy in loving individual persons, sharing friendship and the simple pleasures of human life, and appreciating the small rehabilitation victories for persons with disabilities. It affirms wonder at children learning in pre-school, or adults treading fearfully through the pages of their G.E.D. workbook. Those who dare to say "Yes" to life are nurturers rejoicing in the goodness of creation and the dignity of human striving.

Resistance also is an act of worship. When we first look, resistance seems to be the stuff of activists and prayer seems reserved for contemplatives. If we look more closely, however, we see that real prayer is active engagement with our own doubts, unbeliefs, the evil and good of the world, and with the divine. When we look at resistance anew, we see it differently. Resistance then appears to us to be a form of prayer, a spiritual event. Why? Because genuine resistance is not based on results. Christian resistance finds its rationale in rootedness in the Lord, the Lord of Life, not in success or failure or even the usefulness so prized by our culture. Resistance is an Easter proclamation in a world that cannot see beyond Calvary.

When we resist the engines of darkness and the forces of violent death, therefore, we are proclaiming that God alone is God, an act of transforming faith. Witnessing to the divine is at the heart of a lifestyle of resistance. It proclaims to a world where violence and death are king and queen that our God is a God of the living. Our God is active amidst a death-fixated world. That assertion is itself an act of faith and prayer. Moreover, the awesomeness of the reality we proclaim should drop us to our knees in reverence for the divine in our midst—working, transforming, energizing, and converting death to life. Resistance, therefore, can be a school for prayer.

One footnote on resistance: When we resist—without using violence or weapons of death, without resort to power in ways recognizable to our enemies—their reaction will be hostile, violent, and destructive! It was true for Jesus, and is true for those who dare to respond to his call to discipleship. To live this resistance will demand two things: faith and the support of communities of faithful believers like ourselves. Our faith assures us, with the prophet Jeremiah, that God will make us "a fortified city, a pillar of iron, a wall of brass against the whole land." "They will fight against you," Jeremiah is told, "but not prevail over you, for I am with you to deliver you, says the LORD" (Jer 1:18-19). The communities of faith around us embody the presence and protection of the Lord for us in many ways. In Nouwen's words:

> If life is going to be harder for those who say "No" to war and "Yes" to life, how then can Christian resisters and nonviolent peacemakers stay alive in this world? The simple answer is: together....Resistance which makes for peace is not so much the effort of brave and courageous individuals as the work of the community of faith. Individual people, even the best and the strongest, will soon be exhausted and discouraged, but a community of resistance can persevere even when its members have their moments of weakness and despair. Peacemaking can be a lasting work only when we live and work together.[22]

Thus, our consideration of a lifestyle of resistance on the path of justice draws us to more deeply understand the connection between justice and community, between justice and love. In simple words it says, we can resist the forces of darkness in only one way: together!

The Path of Love

If isolation is a driving force behind the world of darkness, then we might well expect that its opposite, real community, would be central to living in the light. As I indicated at the start of this chapter, to love tenderly we must find our way down a path of love with a community of sisters and brothers who are themselves committed to the same journey. Of course, there are many kinds of communities; among them are families, neighborhoods, rural towns, students in a class, coworkers, religious communities, and church parishes. Our concern here is not just with any communities, but with those communities that enable us to walk the path of justice. As we saw in the last chapter, this means finding and building communities facing the world, communities of resistance to injustice in all three sectors, communities that support our commitment to **faithjustice**.

Most of us will find this support from our spouses and families. Others will find such communities among groups of coworkers, friends in the Lord, prayer support groups, religious congregations, or church parishes. We embark upon this task for a number of good reasons. First, we ourselves need this kind of community, especially those of us committed to creating a more just world. Second, the justice we seek must be embodied in the communities to which we belong or those communities themselves become part of the problem of injustice. Third, communities of resistance are important to countering the engines of darkness in our world, countersigns to the world's competition, domination, isolation, exploitation, and mythology.

If community were just focused on meeting my own needs, then endorsing community building would be a kind of consumerist venture, for what the individual can get out of it. I hear that criticism from religious who say, "Well, no, I don't have time to go to community meetings because we need to be involved in the ministry." Or, when invited to consider a simpler community lifestyle, without servants and in a poorer neighborhood, they respond, "I don't have time to play house." Without the benefit of reflection on the triadic insight, they fail to realize that this engagement with one another in and about community living and with questions of our lifestyle as communities is addressing our world. Such supportive communities can be what theologian Roger Haight calls, "public institutions of grace," without which "the individual will scarcely survive the discouragement of constant defeat."[23] Failing that, we simply duplicate right at home the world's patterns of domination, oppression, and exploitation. And so questions of community building become intimately tied to doing justice, at least when building communities facing the world. These are communities for whom the realities of global and neighborhood justice and injustice are part of their lives together.

What might these communities look like? What themes, contours, directions, and questions ought to characterize them? How might we reflect more deeply upon their contribution to the development of **faithjustice**? I would like to suggest six points for consideration, set against the background of the forces of darkness developed in the last chapter and enriched by several insights into communities and peacemaking, again from Henri Nouwen.[24] Nouwen's approach begins with an analysis that roots the domination of the forces of injustice, war, and violent death in our own wounds and needs and fears. Community, he argues, is or should be at the heart of the way of life, not death. I would like to explain this more in full and develop key themes of what it means to walk on the path of love.

Such communities encourage and support, understand and inspire our living ways. Several moments seem critical to this aspect of finding and building communities of resistance and support. It begins in storytelling. William Newell explains from a study of small faith communities working for justice:

> As we come to the end of this brief, incomplete survey, it seems clear that "listening to story" has been a significant part of the processes of nearly all the groups interviewed. Listening to and valuing the plurality of gifts and religious traditions, attempting to integrate them into work for a more vibrant and just community life—these constitute a spirituality deeply rooted in the U.S. experience.[25]

In describing one such group, Newell notes, "The people realize they have something to say; something is going on in their lives worth listening to, something worth hearing and repeating."[26] This has been my own experience and that of many others whom I know in such communities. Each year as the community begins, sometimes with personnel changes, the members take a weekend away to share their stories with one another. They exchange abbreviated autobiographies and provide insights into what is currently important in their lives. In so doing, they begin the bonding that is essential to living together and dealing with anything of substance during the year ahead.

An expansion of this critical moment occurs in what educator Paulo Freire calls "dialogue." Thomas Groome explains that Freire considered there to be five requirements for such dialogue. Freire clarified these in the very process of working with adult learners in Latin America. First, real dialogue requires a profound love for the world and for people. Second, dialogue requires humility on the part of the participants. By "the naming of the world" they are constantly re-creating it, which cannot be an act of arrogance, Freire insists. Third, dialogue requires an intense faith in the human person and in the human "power to make and remake, to create and re-create...." This, says Groome, "is not a naive faith, however, that ignores failure, but one that refuses to accept failure or human refusal as the final verdict." Rather, it must lead to a relationship that Freire calls "mutual trust between the dialoguers." That faith is more the result of dialogue than its prerequisite. Fourth, Groome explains,

> [D]ialogue requires hope, a hope that is aware of our incompleteness but is determined not to settle for silence or escape from reality. It is an active hope, but not an impatient one that gives up or continues only if there are results. Freire warns, "As the encounter of men seeking to be more fully human, dialogue cannot be carried on in a climate of hopelessness."[27]

Lastly, Freire indicates that authentic dialogue presupposes critical thinking. Groome adds from his own experience of shared Christian praxis in religious education that such "dialogue is not only among the participants but also between the participants and God." In his experience, the very listening to others in a community of dialogue often causes the other participants to find "our inner dialogue merging into dialogue with God."[28]

For Christian communities, one story takes preeminence over the others, what Larry Rasmussen calls "the normative story," the Jesus story. Without it, Rasmussen argues, "the community as a Christian community ceases to exist."[29] The Jesus story grounds the community, molds people's identities and their sense of the world and all reality.

> Powerful stories—like the Jesus story—create a basic orientation for those who are drawn into them. They shape our perception of life and hone our sensitivities. They help form commitments and nurture loyalties. They yield transforming insight. And they solicit our own involvement in pursuing the story further.[30]

In this sharing of stories and the shaping of the community by the Jesus story, we find ourselves accepted as loved, warts and all. The community is a sign of how our God loves: gratuitously. Such loving confirms us in loving first as well. This is the initial building block in the special care for the poor.

Such communities permit vulnerability and teach compassion. So much of our culture glosses over the reality of human vulnerability. It even encourages us, through accumulating wealth and popular myth-making, to deny that reality, even to ourselves. Our task then is to build families, work groups, and support and prayer communities that are profoundly countercultural in the sense that they acknowledge, implicitly and explicitly, our vulnerability and shared humanity. We need to affirm that we are what Nouwen calls, "a fellowship of the weak."[31] From our experiences of story-telling and true dialogue, we first learn to dismantle the demilitarized zones and non-aggression pacts that humans erect as easily as nations.

Our families and communities then become places where we compassionately help one another to sense and **feel** the "this is mine" and "I alone" whenever it arises in us to protect our own vulnerability. Rather than fear the stares of others who are somehow alien to that vulnerability, members in such communities should feel supported by the loving glances of others who share their brokenness. Mary Ann Fatula describes this through the experiences of Jean Vanier:

> Carl Jung once remarked that he could not understand how Christians can see Jesus in the poor around them, but not in their own poverty. In response, Vanier comments that no one of us finds it easy to admit our poverty. In our own ways we each avoid coming face to face with our weakness. "We prefer to live in the illusions of our perfection....We always want to appear good and perfect." ...But "healing cannot take place until our illusions have been exposed and we acknowledge our human reality...."

> ...Vanier's experience of living in community with the handicapped at l'Arche, however, taught him that he didn't need to bear the burden of his weakness alone. With the love and support of the community, he no longer found it necessary to pretend, even to himself, that all was light within him.[32]

This positive common experience of shared hurts enables us to be free of the compulsion to feign invulnerability. It also deepens our compassion for those suffering in the grip of poverty and also in the velvet slavery of success and wealth.

One key to building this compassionate environment will be prayer with one another, sharing our honest recognition of need for God and for human support. Such prayerful bonding must occur even when we feel unable to pray, too tired or frustrated by the injustice we encounter even to raise our arms in supplication. Then we need others' voices and hands like Moses physically supported in prayer by Aaron and Hur (Ex 17:12).

Such learning communities also must allow us to encounter and transcend our own anger in social ministry, no matter how slowly and painfully it passes. Christine Gaylor and Annelle Fitzpatrick explain:

> Such a community can help the individual understand that anger is not necessarily a stumbling block to growth; it can at times be an appropriate and justifiable emotion. Scripture tells us that even the Lord grew angry on occasion. Indeed, we believe that anger, if reflected on rather than merely vented, can be a stepping stone to another level of consciousness. Prolonged and blind anger, however, can be damaging to an individual's well-being. If persons are to continue to function and grow, their anger must be "touched," their personhood affirmed, and the anguish experienced in the depths of their being must be met with more than a patronizing and hollow "I understand."
>
> We propose that the experience of being accepted in spite of one's anger can only be achieved by bonding with individuals who share the vision, dream the dream, and survive with the wounds. In such a community of survivors, there is no need to convert or defend, and explanation is easier because members of the community share not only an ideological affinity but a spiritual interpretation of the events that brought them together.[33]

Gaylor and Fitzpatrick underscore the importance of both the individual and communal stories shared in compassion and the normative story of Jesus. From these, then, flows the support for learning the ways of light, for learning how to live free of the domination of the forces of darkness, specifically our anger.

Such communities must also enable the experience of giving and receiving mercy and forgiveness for the hurts inflicted on one another in family or community and for the barriers erected in the name of self-protection. This, too, is part of tasting and learning the reconciliation offered by the Lord, critical to supportive community, and essential to building the reign of God as well. If we cannot experience this life-giving reconciliation in family and community, where can our world learn it?

Such communities offer an environment for discerning the Spirit out of which we move in action for justice. How do I know that I am not playing the "lone ranger" in my work for justice, like too many others before me? How can I be sure that the good I do is for the right reason, not driven by the engines of darkness or Nouwen's "ways of death"? Besides my own passion, prayer, reflection, experience, and connection to the **anawim** and to the tradition, submission to the community's discernment provides an important assist to my own. This requires, of course, that I belong to a community facing the world, a community of resistance which is itself standing with the poor.

For many people engaged in the pursuit of justice, just such a local community gathered in prayer is a privileged place for discerning God's action in us. "We feel that the community of faith that we are when we gather together is the primary locus of God's word to us," one community member commented, even the scriptures being secondary.[34] Larry Rasmussen would grant the critical role of the local community, but argue that one needed corrective is membership in the universal church itself.

> This translates as an openness to, and exchange with, other understandings of the Jesus story and other styles of the Christian life. These can check the persistent tendencies of a close Christian community to be sectarian, to identify its particular community as "the Church."[35]

Rasmussen's point is well taken, and the larger church should be a backdrop for our discernment in any smaller community. We must note, however, that in church history the smaller Christian community with passionate commitment to gospel values often has provided the important prophetic edge to the church's own institutional tendency to domesticate the gospel. Only years later has the mainstream church acknowledged the truth of the prophetic stance. There is then a tension between submission to the local and universal faith communities; but both are valuable to discerning our action for justice in concrete historical situations. The privilege of the local community is partly in its knowledge of who I am, what my own story is, our dialogue in faith, and its commitment to being a community facing the world in solidarity with the poor.

Such communities will be notable as a milieu of hospitality and peacefulness. In contrast to the drivenness produced by the engines of darkness in the world and Nouwen's wants and needs in the human heart, communities of resistance will take a step back from the madness. They will be places of hospitality. Their members will find, create, and celebrate peacefulness. In the concrete, this will take a number of forms, a few of which are mentioned here. First, the resisting community will be noted for celebration and joy, nurturing life and goodness by affirmation, gratitude, graciousness, and laughter.

In its tempo, this kind of community will welcome the "non-productive" in the face of the myths of productivity and getting ahead. This begins with so-called non-productive times and events: the celebration of birthdays and anniversaries of all types, savoring large and small victories and grieving over losses, welcoming friends and neighbors, and enjoying a holiday or vacation together. Central to this experience will be the meal, that crucial time for family or community when days and lives are shared on a regular basis. The community will also welcome the so-called non-producers into its midst: there will be a place for elders, for persons with disabilities, for the sick, for foreigners and refugees, and for poor persons. Hospitality was to be a mark of the Hebrew covenant community, welcoming the widow, the orphan, and the stranger into full membership in the community. So, too, there must be hospitality in today's community of faith. It begins in a fundamental openness to others' views, experiences, and remembering. The kind of listening discussed above is at the heart of this hospitality.

The community also will develop what Patricia Natali calls a rhythm of "withdrawal and return":

> As we see in the Scripture, Moses is drawn into the desert and encounters the "burning bush" only to leave the desert and become the leader of the people. Jesus goes to pray in the wilderness, goes to the mountaintop and the desert. But all these withdrawals are temporary. There is a return to a fuller and greater service to God's people.[36]

The community then takes its time away, but always with the sense of its mission. In Natali's experience with groups that kept their faces toward the world, a liturgical group led people to volunteer with the homeless, a work support group resulted in action for justice in the workplace, and a prayer support group began work with the poor in a housing project. There is withdrawal, she writes, but "the withdrawal is for the sake of the return."[37] Withdrawal, however, there must be, discovering God within oneself and in the community in ways that reveal God more clearly active in the world.

Such communities, however small, are the seeds of a great harvest of *faithjustice*. One experience of many of us involved in the struggle to build a more compassionate world is that there are so few of us. There often seem to be so few individuals and communities committed to building the reign of God. In contrast, there seem to be so many dedicated to the ways of war, violence, wealth, or success, and so many others ready to sign on with them. Joseph Hacala of the Campaign for Human Development told me this story of statistics. He was speaking to an audience in the days before the Gulf War and bemoaned the fact that only 16 percent of Americans were opposed to proposed U.S. invasion of Iraq. A woman yelled from the audience, "It's down to 9 percent now!"

Henri Nouwen calls this the "illusion of statistics" and reminds us that the way of the gospel and Christian history teach us the wonderful impact of the few on the many. Jesus himself, the twelve, and those sent out two by two are all lessons in the ways of God. Those ways confound the wise and powerful and delight the children and the **anawim**. Our communities then must be places where we retell the Jesus story to one another as encouragement in the face of the statistics. Even more, we must remind one another, as Nouwen writes, that pursuit of justice and peace is a privileged example of the wisdom of the gospel:

> The small groups of "disobedient" people who here and there jump the fences of nuclear weapons facilities, climb on board nuclear submarines, or put their bodies in front of nuclear transports are trying to wake us up to a reality we continue to ignore or deny. Their small number should not mislead us. Throughout history the truth has seldom, if ever, been spoken by majorities. Statistics are not the way truth becomes known. The prophets of Israel, Jesus and his few disciples, and the small bands of men and women throughout history are there to make us wonder if "these crazy peaceniks" might after all not be as important for our conversion today as St. Francis and his followers were seven centuries ago. Their loud, clear, and often dramatic "No" has to make us wonder what kind of "No" **we** are called to speak.[38]

We must remind ourselves and our communities continually of the seed that must die before the harvest is possible. Our few lives, families and communities of resistance, small projects, and great dreams must be planted in the soil of history in order for the reign of God to blossom. This is the hope we share in our communities for the resurrection of justice.

All that we do in these communities then follows the pattern of death and resurrection. That is why the celebration of the eucharist is one irreplaceable symbol of our work and our hopes. As Jesuit Superior

General Peter-Hans Kolvenbach put it recently to a conference of people working for justice and peace:

> To the Eucharist we bring all our efforts to tear down the barriers of race, gender, class and nationality, all our struggles for justice. And from the Eucharist, celebrated in the fullness of its reality and mystery, we must draw the strength and the love that sustains our common and united commitment to transform the unjust structures of society.[39]

The eucharist patterns the life of Jesus, from death in failure to triumph in resurrection. As such, it reiterates our own small efforts which by the same power of God can be multiplied into a harvest of justice and peace. Only God can do it.

Such communities tutor the world in the ways to justice and peace. Despite their failures and fragility, despite the disappearance of one or another community of resistance, their very existence and their ways of being community have an effect in the larger world of systems and structures. Communities facing the world provide a simple witness, nothing flashy, to dialogue, to compassion, and to forgiveness and reconciliation. These are all lessons needed if we are ever to heal Northern Ireland, the Middle East, South Africa, Central America, or the great chasm between rich and poor in our own country.

In their struggle for day-to-day life and love, families and communities committed to **faithjustice** grow slowly as the flowers grow, as life does. They remind us that the reign of God comes gradually, bit-by-bit, involving every place of work, every public decision, every private expenditure, and every moment of our lives. No person, place, or power is exempt from the challenge, and each must be enlisted for the long haul of God's project in history.

To sum up this discussion, communities with their faces toward the world, communities that enable us to walk the way of resistance, must hear Jesus say to them:

> *Everyone will be salted with fire. Salt is good, but if salt becomes insipid, with what will you restore its flavor? Keep salt in yourselves and you will have peace with one another (Mk 9:49–50).*

In these few words Jesus reminds us of important themes that must define and animate such communities: friendship, commitment, suffering, and passion for justice. Salt shared was the Hebrew sign of friendship and alliance. Travelers gathered at the oasis after a day of journeying shared salt with one another. Used in the sacrifices of the scriptures, salt also was a sign of the permanence of the covenant between Yahweh and the people of Israel. The Hebrew "covenant of salt" is translated in Numbers 18:19 as the *"inviolable covenant."*[40] In our **faithjustice** communities, then, salt first symbolizes the commitment we have to one another for mutual support on the journey. It then recalls our covenant with the Lord's poor, peaceful and inviolable.

Salting **with fire** reminds us, as Jesus warns his disciples, of the purification we disciples will experience through persecution and suffering for the reign of God.[41] We who have looked at the power and pervasiveness of the forces of darkness in the world and in ourselves know what Jesus promises. We have experienced the narrowness and steepness of the path we must travel. Salting with fire then reiterates that we must be simultaneously at peace with one another, sharing one another's suffering, and on fire with the passion of God for the poor who hold a privileged place in God's heart. With such fiery salt, God can season the world.

The Path of Reverence

If we are to walk humbly with our God, if we are to walk in the light, then our pilgrimage also must follow a path of reverence enlightened by prayer and also by a renewed sense of sabbath. It has been clear from the points developed earlier in this chapter that prayer is woven throughout a life of **faithjustice** lived in the light. Often, early in our activist lives, prayer seems a luxury and many abandon it...for a while. Then, prayer becomes necessary, essential. Prayer is critical to seeing the connections between systemic, communal, and personal justice and injustice. Prayer helps us to find our way between the extremes of anger and guilt, power and powerlessness, and success and failure. To contemplate Jesus in the normative story, to listen and dialogue with others in community, and to have the hope and courage to live a life of resistance all demand that we enter into the mystery of God in Christ and in ourselves.

There are many ways of praying, of course, even for individuals and communities committed to remaking the world. For individuals, Jim McGinnis suggests a prayer of solidarity, "accompanying" others in prayer in the course of a day and letting them know by a letter or phone call that we have been with them in spirit.[42] For communities in the process of discerning any course of action, John Haughey describes three functions for prayer, "a disposing, a disclosing, and finally a confirming..."[43] Prayer first disposes the group to be about the process of consideration and deliberation in greater harmony. Then the group prays to disclose the course of action to be taken. Finally, prayer can confirm the tradition, the group's identity, individual or group experience, or the decision.

Another view of prayer in the group, Haughey says, is that it is "intentionally use-less." "It is its own reason for being done," he adds. "It is done because God is God."[44] While this might seem very different from the use of prayer for disposing, disclosing, and confirming group decisions, Haughey sees the attitude of use-less prayer as complementary. From our earlier discussions, we can see that Haughey's emphasis here is consistent with the crucial withdrawal dynamic of community life. Just as it is important for a community to withdraw regularly from the justice and peace fray, so too is an attitude about prayer's use-less-ness. Both are countercultural to our pragmatic society. Too often we go to prayer to find an answer, solve a problem, cure a friend, or otherwise make something happen. Here, in this kind of use-less prayer, we encounter the God within ourselves and our community who is also the God operative in society. We do so without pragmatic purpose and yet we are enriched by the revelation of God's truth and our own and, as Nouwen notes, our own deepening solidarity with all people.

Relating prayer directly to our journey on the path of justice, Nouwen underscores the importance of the increasing revelation of our own truth in prayer. The more we see ourselves reflected in the face of God, the more easily we can recognize our own woundedness and how much our needs for attention and praise shape our own behavior. We see our own desperate search for love, driven by our needs and wounds, that so often turns into its opposites. This "milieu of needs and wounds," Nouwen says, is home for those who hate peace and create injustice. When we enter into prayer, we have to "rip off the mask of deception" to see ourselves. We must see our own implication in the making of war and injustice, our own drivenness by needs and wounds, in order to become peacemakers and to do justice. Otherwise, what we try to do for justice or peace is done out of panic or fear, generating the opposite of what we desire.

Jesus, therefore, offers us a different milieu, a dwelling place in himself in prayer. There we find true peace. There we experience ourselves as being loved first, and that love experience gives birth to peacemaking. We enter into this dwelling place by our prayer, experience ourselves as first-being-loved, and realize that only in God are we free of the needs and wounds and fears that motor war and injustice.

> For us to work for justice and peace and really be activists in the good sense of the word is to do it not because we need to prove to ourselves or anybody that we are worth loving. Rather, it is because we are so in touch with our belovedness that we are free to act according to the truth and say "no" to injustice and say "yes" when we see justice and peace.[45]

We can only say we are for justice, work for peace, and be real peacemakers when the powers of darkness have no further power over us. That freedom is the gift of God given in prayer.

Prayer also is related to guilt and compassion, concerns we have discussed before. One version of the burnout experience says, "I can't carry this burden anymore." It implies that compassion is not a real human possibility. Underlying this, Nouwen argues, is an illusion that claims that ideally we should be able to carry one another's burden, eliminate human pain, and save the world. Otherwise, why did we accept the call to follow this Christ? The problem is not that we cannot do it all, he says, but that we want to do it all. The answer to this problem is not to do what we can and leave the rest to God. Instead, it is, "You cannot do anything, but God can do everything in you."

What this means is that God has drawn all human sin and suffering into God's own self in Christ Jesus. The all-compassionate God has suffered fully with us and really understands our pain. There is no limit to God's solidarity with us, again, in Christ Jesus. "Every human attempt to be compassionate independent of Christ is doomed to failure. The discipline of compassion only makes sense as an expression of discipleship."[46] We do not just follow Christ as some good example. Rather, God's compassion in Christ is the source of all human compassion, which in turn reflects the divine compassion. Without Christ, compassion is impossible; with Christ, it is limitless and his burden is light.

> When we care for a lonely man, teach an ignorant child, spend time with a sad woman, offer food to the hungry, and work for justice and peace in our house, city, state, country or world, we are in fact giving visibility to God's boundless compassion. In Christ, there is no place for guilt feelings or complaints. In Christ, we can "do a little thing" while doing much, we can show care without being crushed and we can face the pains of the world without becoming gloomy, depressed or doomsday prophets... As long as we act as if the task to save the world rested on our own shoulders, we have to ignore a lot of pain or we become

depressed. But when we begin to realize that we can do nothing ourselves but everything in Christ, our solidarity with our neighbor can be
a joyful solidarity, a solidarity through which the great compassion of
God can bring new life into the hearts of people.[47]

In reality, what occurs is the unmasking of the illusion of a false
activism and a restoration of the priority of prayer.

Prayer, though, is not then "romantic, sweet, or easy," says Nouwen,
not a cop-out from reality. Rather, it connects us to a God who self-
reveals as the God of our neighbor. Prayer thus makes our love for
God a love that embraces all people, just as Jesus entered into solidarity
with the suffering world. Then, through this mystery we come to understand why the second great commandment is like the first and "prayer
is the mother and father, brother and sister of all compassion."[48]

Prayer is also directly related to the value placed in the path of justice upon fidelity. In a world so enamored of success and results, fidelity is divine gift. It cuts against the cultural grain. In prayer we learn
fidelity. We see it first in God's fidelity to humanity, which remains
constant for us even if we are unfaithful (2 Tim 2:13). We see this
fidelity in God's special care for the **anawim**, for whom Yahweh
remains responsible even when the people and their rulers fail to care.

In our prayer, we come to see this same responsibility reflected in
the life and ministry of Jesus of Nazareth. As we watch Jesus and learn
of his dual passion for the will of God and the reign of God, we also
see that he is the faithful Son. When the leadership of the people line
up against him, when the crowds cry out for his death, and when even
his disciples desert him, he remains faithful. As we watch and meditate,
we realize that his fidelity persists despite his own desires—*"take this cup
away from me,"* Luke 22:42. His fidelity persists despite the apparent
failure of his mission and the pain and suffering of his death.

For us, then, we learn in prayer of the special fidelity of God to us
and to the poor, and so we are enabled to live in that same fidelity. And
we learn from the fidelity of Jesus to be faithful to our own commitments to justice and peace despite our desires for comfort, relevance,
or power and despite apparent failure and the suffering of our journey.
Our fidelity then is itself an act of reverence for the God of fidelity.

To walk on the path of reverence we must also rediscover the genius
and meaning of sabbath. In a presentation on social justice in the early
eighties, activist and educator Edward van Merrienboer explained that
a surprising theme from his conversations with a number of social justice educators was the importance of the sabbath. Since I first heard
that talk, the truth of van Merrienboer's insight has become increasing-

ly important in reflecting on ways of survival and renewal in the struggle for **faithjustice**. In essence, celebrating the sabbath, in whatever form, is about, first, taking some time away for ourselves and for God. To do so, we must step back from work.

At its most simple level, taking the sabbath is a matter of rudimentary good health, e.g., "He or she who fights and runs away lives to fight another day." It reflects a pragmatic recognition that we are not invincible, that we cannot work fifteen hours a day for seven days a week for fifty-two weeks a year...not for long. This, too, is a lesson that sometimes takes activists years to master. We work through weekends and holidays and cut short our vacations, if we take them at all. But many of us eventually learn, or our spouses and families urge upon us, or a health crisis brings the point home more suddenly and rudely.

At a more reflective level, taking the sabbath also has meaning for the work we do and the people we serve. What does it say to the poor and to the rich about life and the significance of family and friends if we take no time to appreciate the goodness of nature or of those around us? What are we modeling about human dignity and community if our own lifestyle is a driven one, devoid of real enjoyment? Taking care of ourselves and of others is an important way to communicate values which we hold to be important to human life and to changing the world.

At yet another level, the concept of the sabbath takes us back to other considerations earlier in this chapter and in chapter one about drivenness. The sabbath invites us to test ourselves on the drivenness scale. This consideration can lead us to discern what spirit in ourselves is dominating our actions. Is it darkness or light, freedom or compulsion? If I can never play ball in the park on Sunday afternoon or go fishing on the bayou or fly a kite with the kids or go to a concert with friends, where am I? Is there something within me that says I cannot relax while people suffer anywhere in the world? Celebrating the sabbath is an offset to the drivenness of guilt, fear, or anger. It celebrates creation as gift, life as "very good," and that the gifts of creation are meant to be enjoyed.

Most importantly, the sabbath is a profound acknowledgment at the spiritual level that God is God and not me. The ultimate victory over injustice that is resurrection comes about by the power of God, not by my powers. Taking the sabbath, then, is an affirmation of crucial truths about reality. It proclaims to the world and to ourselves that God cares. In fact, God's caring about these problems long antedates my own; but I forget that so often. Taking the sabbath means that I can trust enough to hand this business of justice and peace over to God and others. This letting-go can be a profoundly faith-filled act for many of us. We can actually say, I don't have to be available by the phone twenty-four hours a day. Handing whatever over to God also is an admission of my own limits, a truth that I will face in my own dying:

> A fifth quality of the courageous and patient advocate of justice is a confident and serene acknowledgment of the limits of one's capabilities, energy, time, and wisdom. Magnanimity is not the same as the effort to ape God by becoming responsible for everything that happens on the face of the earth. Because we human beings are finite and limited creatures, human courage includes the ability to accept our honest limits. Daring and endurance will acquire true focus to the extent that these limits are accepted. Such acceptance is the beginning of courage truly to be oneself and truly to give oneself to the struggle for justice.[49]

The sabbath thus gives us a perspective in modesty, one that situates my gifts and efforts in the context of the larger plan and action of God in transforming the world.

The final aspect of this understanding of sabbath is that it is an acknowledgment that the way of Jesus Christ was right. Jesus operated out of no five-year plan, had no multimedia program, no cable network, not even a stadium appearance. His pattern was like the ways of life we reflected on above: slowly growing, gentle measures, small steps. He did not choose the loud, violent, powerful ways of darkness and death. Even after the resurrection, his approach was modest. He spent some time with a few disciples, ate with friends, went fishing, walked on the road to Emmaus with others, and went off by himself to pray. So, too, when we celebrate the sabbath in the company of friends and loved ones, enjoy a good book, listen to a symphony, or take time for daily prayer or an annual retreat, ultimately it's an acknowledgment that the way of Jesus is right. And living by that way will bring the reign of God to fulfillment.

The Way

It should be clear both from the discussions in this volume and from our own experience that there are strong forces against which we pit ourselves in the struggle to make this a more just, peaceful, and compassionate world. In the process described in chapter three, we identified five underlying engines of darkness that affect us individually, communally, and systemically. These were competition, domination, consumption, isolation, and myths, especially the myth of invulnerability.

Against those forces, this final chapter suggests that our pilgrimage requires us to walk three paths—of justice, love, and reverence. Along these paths the signposts have names like simple lifestyle, fidelity, hope, courage, resistance, community, laughter, hospitality, prayer, and the sabbath. These will enable us to move personally, communally, and systemically to create a more just world, with special care for the **anawim** of Yahweh. What we have also learned implicitly and saw in the triadic insight into darkness is that the three paths are one. To do justice we must love tenderly and walk humbly with our God.

As sometimes happens, brief poetry can say far more than a wealth of prose. On the back of his ordination card in 1975, a friend named Peter Byrne wrote the following. In doing so he expressed the heart of what this book has been about:

> We are simply asked
> to make gentle our bruised world
> to tame its savageness
> to be compassionate of all
>   including oneself
> then with the time left over
>   to repeat the ancient tale and
>   go the way of God's foolish ones
>   Peter Byrne, SJ

NOTES

Introduction

1. Center of Concern literature describes itself as "an independent, inter-disciplinary team engaged in social analysis, theological reflection, policy advocacy, and public education on issues of peace and justice."

2. See for example, discussion in Fred Kammer, S.J., *Doing Faithjustice* (Mahwah, N.J.: Paulist Press, 1991), pp. 168–181.

3. Joseph P. Daoust, S.J., "The Social Dimension of Ministry for the Reign of God," Address to the Thirtieth Annual National Assembly of the Conference of Major Superiors of Men, St. Louis, Missouri, August 13, 1986, p. 23.

4. Joe Holland and Peter Henriot, S.J., *Social Analysis: Linking Faith and Justice* (Maryknoll: Orbis Books, 1983), p. 8.

5. Anthony J. Tambasco, "Option for the Poor," in *The Deeper Meaning of Economic Life* (Washington, D.C.: Georgetown University Press, 1986), R. Bruce Douglass (ed.), pp 37–55 at 41.

6. Francisco Ivern, S.J., "The Future of Faith and Justice: A Critical Review of Decree Four," in *Studies in the Spirituality of Jesuits*, Vol. 14, No. 5, November, 1982, p. 10.

Chapter One

1. Jody Shearer, "Avoiding Burnout: Keeping a Vision While Volunteering," in *Southern Perspectives*, Spring, 1990, pp. 3-6, at 3-4.

2. Cited by Richard L. Smith in "An American Reply: '*Burn-Out*' Poses Deeper Questions," *Studies in the Spirituality of Jesuits*, Vol. X, No. 1, January, 1978, pp. 21-31, at 29.

3. Ibid., p. 29.

4. Judy Cassidy, "Compassion Fatigue," in *Health Progress*, Vol. 72, No. 1, January-February, 1991, pp. 54-64.

5. Over ten years ago, I wrote an article on burnout among Jesuit social activists, which provides the basis for the first part of this chapter. Research since then has widened and deepened the analysis and appreciation of burnout. Cf. Alfred C. Kammer, S.J., "'Burn-out'—Contemporary Dilemma for the Jesuit Social Activist,'" *Studies in the Spirituality of Jesuits*, Vol. X, No. 1, January, 1978, pp. 1-20.

6. Significant correlations also exist between burnout and alcoholism, mental illness, marital conflict, and suicide. See "Burned-Out," by Christina Maslach, in *Human Behavior* magazine, September, 1976, pp. 18-22. See, also, "Consultant Burnout," by Michael C. Mitchell, in *The 1977 Annual Handbook for Group Facilitators*, pp. 143-46.

7. Fran Osseo-Asare, "The End of the Wick," in *Sojourners*, Vol. 8, No. 6, June, 1979, p. 19.

8. Christina Maslach and Susan E. Jackson, "Burnout in Organizational Settings," *Applied Social Psychology Annual*, Vol. 5, 1984, pp. 133-135.

9. Sister Mary Vincentia Joseph, D.S.W., "The Roots of Burnout: Implications for Church Ministries," in *Church Personnel Issues*, January 1988, pp. 1-6, at 1.

10. James J. Gill, S.J., M.D., "Burnout: A Growing Threat in Ministry," in *Human Development*, Vol. 1, No. 2, Summer 1980, pp. 21-27, at 22.

11. Christina Maslach's stages, as described in Gill, *Ibid.*, p. 23.

12. They include: physical fatigue, exhaustion; insomnia; body tension; frequent sickness; backache or neckache; increased perspiration; migraine headaches; serious illness; worry about work or clients; difficulty making decisions; guilt feelings about work performance; preoccupation with problems; griping, cynicism; feeling frustrated, overwhelmed; loss of enthusiasm, feeling of stagnation; anger, resentment; blaming others and organization; accident prone; hostile thinking and speech; yelling; impatient; irritated; uncharacteristic behavior; loss of concern for others; treating clients coldly; stereotyping clients; communicating with clients impersonally; reduction of time spent with clients; mechanical performance of duties; excessive intellectualization; repression of feelings. *Ibid.*

13. See Dominic Maruca, S.J., "The Graces of the Third and Fourth Weeks," in *Soundings: A Task Force on Social Consciousness and Ignatian Spirituality* (Center of Concern, 1974), pp. 25-27.

14. Cf. Colleen Scanlon, R.N.C., and Mary Packard, R.N., "Seeing to One's Self," *Health Progress*, Vol. 72, No. 1, January-February, 1991, pp. 50-53; and "Burnout Price of Working in Epidemic," *AIDSLINE*, Vol. 4, No. 1, Spring, 1992, pp. 3-4.

15. Richard P. Johnson, Ph.D., "Easing the Burden of Stress," *Health Progress*, Vol. 72, No. 1, January-February, 1991, pp. 56-59.

16. *Ibid.*, at 58.

17. The person with this awareness thinks in terms of change and in utopias. He or she sharply contrasts what is happening in his or her work with what **could** happen. He or she discovers that what happens in society has causes which are artificial in the sense that they are products of human intent or structures. Therefore, what happens is indefensible and intolerable and creates new anguish and lack of confidence in what the reformer personally is doing. Francisco Ornelas, S.J., "A Reflection by Mexican Jesuits on Their Experience," *Studies in the Spirituality of Jesuits*, January, 1978, Vol. X, No. 1, pp. 32-36.

18. "Annals of the Law—The Liberty of Every Man," Richard Harris, *The New Yorker*, November 3, 1975, p. 55.

19. Christine C. Gaylor, C.S.J., and Annelle Fitzpatrick, C.S.J., describe six-stages of consciousness-expansion in becoming aware of and eventually taking a stand against structural injustices. "The Stages of Consciousness Raising," in *Human Development*, Vol. 8, No. 3, Fall 1987, pp. 6-11.

20. Cf. Patrick Kerans, *Sinful Social Structures* (New York: Paulist Press, 1974).

21. I was angry at the province, at the parish, at white people, at the corporations, at the United States, at the pope. I was angry at basically everyone (including myself). I justified my anger. I told myself that all these "others" should be more just and should convert from their ways. Many reacted to my anger with their own anger. Others just avoided me. Still others feared me.

Michael H. Crosby, O.F.M., Cap., *Spirituality of the Beatitudes* (Maryknoll, N.Y.: Orbis Books, 1981), p. 157.

22. Loughlin Sofield, S.T., Carroll Juliano, S.H.C.J., and Rosine Hammett, C.S.C., *Design for Wholeness* (Notre Dame, IN: Ave Maria Press, 1990), p. 20.

23. For Gaylor and Fitzpatrick, *op. cit.*, at p. 10, anger is the fifth stage of consciousness-expansion. To survive, the person needs the healing and acceptance of others who have "been there."

24. If we cannot be angry then we cannot really be compassionate either. If my heart goes out to people who are suffering, then I must be angry with those who make them suffer....So sometimes I must be angry. Sometimes I must share God's anger. The bible is full of God's anger, which we tend to find embarrassing at times, rather than helpful to our spiritual lives....It is not a question of hating or blaming or being angry with individuals as such, but of tremendous indignation against a system that creates so much suffering and so much poverty. My suggestion is that the more we have that anger, the closer we are to God.

Albert Nolan, O.P., "Spiritual Growth and the Option for the Poor," in *Church*, Vol. 1, No. 1, Spring 1985, pp. 45-48, at 46.

25. Sofield, Juliano, and Hammett summarize steps to deal with anger: (1) Acknowledge and accept the feeling of anger and its intensity. (2) Become calm and think through the situation. (3) Identify the need, want, attack on self-esteem or injustice that has stimulated the anger, and the underlying beliefs causing the anger. (4) Determine how essential is the underlying belief. (5) Decide what action to take to express the anger. (6) Look at the situation and individuals involved in deciding upon the appropriate course of action. (7) Decide to forgive. Loughlin Sofield, S.T., *et al.*, *op. cit.*, pp. 40-41.

26. George B. Wilson, S.J., argues that all of us now belong to a wide range of relationships, "multiple memberships" which shape our own experiences and views and which lead, in families or in religious communities, to "conflicting networks of expectations" and choices. "Where Do We Belong? United States Jesuits and Their Memberships," in *Studies in the Spirituality of Jesuits*, Vol. 21, No. 1, January 1989, p. 1-32, at 8.

27. William L. Bryan, "Preventing **Burnout** in the Public Interest Community," in *The Grantsmanship Center News*, March/April 1981, pp. 15-75, at 21.

28. Gail Sheehy, in her best-seller *Passages*, gives particular stress to the role of mentors in the move of young men and women into their adult careers. Her analysis underscores the problem of a lack of viable models for social activists. (N.Y.: E.P. Dutton & Co., Inc., 1976).

29. Social psychologists Berger and Luckmann describe as **internalization** the transmitting of institutionalized patterns and processes which have been superimposed upon reality. It is the third stage in the genesis and maintenance of social structures, following upon the processes of **externalization** and **objectivation**. Peter Berger and Thomas Luckmann, *The Social Construction of Reality* (Garden City, N.Y.: Doubleday & Co., 1966, Anchor Books Edition, 1967), pp. 47-62.

30. William J. Byron, S.J., "The Social Dimension of Jesuit Group Apostolates," printed in *Proceedings of the New Orleans Province Assembly–Session 5* (1975), p. 60.

31. Gaylor and Fitzpatrick, *op. cit.*, p. 11, see activists often moved to the "creative alienation" of beginning alternative structures to continue the same kind of work—e.g., education or health care. William J. Byron, S.J., returning to this discussion later argued that the "versus" linkages could be converted into hyphens by religious, forging connecting links of reconciliation between rich and poor, black and white, and other divided groups. "Stewardship, Justice, and the Jesuit Purpose in Education," Symposium Paper, Creighton University, Omaha, NB, June 8, 1978, p.7.

32. See the distinction discussed by Charles E. O'Neill, S.J., regarding "faith" and "religion" in "**Acatamiento**: Ignatian Reverence in History and Contemporary Culture," *Studies in the Spirituality of Jesuits*, Vol. 8, No. 1, January, 1976, p. 8.

33. Gustavo Gutierrez, *A Theology of Liberation* (N.Y.: Orbis Books, 1973), p. 136.

34. T. J. McDonnell, "Transubstantiating the Wasteland," *Worship*, Vol. 47, No. 2, February, 1973, pp. 93-99, at 93.

35. McDonnell, *op. cit.*, p. 95.

36. *Ibid.*

37. Noel Barré, S.J., "A Response to the Mexican Jesuits from a French Worker-Priest," in *Studies in the Spirituality of Jesuits*, Vol. 10, No. 1, January, 1978, pp. 37-38, at 38.

38. Gill, *op. cit.*, at p. 24, gives a list of those persons "generally the most vulnerable" to burnout.

39. Joseph, *op. cit.*, p. 24.

40. Note that in a non-empirical discussion of the burnout of public interest staff, nine causes listed include more that focus on the organization and environment than on the persons involved: a) intense external pressures on public interest organizations; b) lack of clear direction in the work environment; c) lack of organizational and personal processes for saying "no"; d) uncertainty of rewards; e) lack of security; f) the illusiveness of success; g) the intensity of the

workplace; h) the Ralph Nader syndrome; and i) lack of appropriate work habits. William L. Bryan, *op. cit.*, pp. 18-22.

41. Joseph, *op. cit.*, pp. 3-4.

42. Priestly Life and Ministry Committee, National Conference of Catholic Bishops, "Reflections on the Morale of Priests," in *Origins*, Vol. 18, No. 31, January 12, 1989, pp. 497-505, at 502.

43. Joseph, *op. cit.*, pp. 4-5.

44. *Ibid.*, p. 5.

45. "Reflections on the Morale of Priests," *op. cit.*, p. 500.

46. Joseph, *op. cit.*, p. 5.

47. Bryan argues that there is need for actually establishing a "public interest profession" which could include skill development and sharing of individual and organizational resources as part of its mandate. *Op. cit.*, p. 72.

48. At the 1989 Solidarity Conference co-sponsored by the U.S. Catholic Conference, Roundtable, the Catholic Rural Life Conference, and the Campaign for Human Development, Frederick Perella of the Diocese of Hartford, and Mary Heidkamp of Louisville, Kentucky, both experienced advocates for social justice, offered a workshop entitled "Staying Well While Doing Good." (March 1, 1989, Washington, D.C.) It included such topics as clear job definitions, goals, personal relationships, time for recreation and exercise, setting limits, and spirituality.

49. Gutierrez, *op. cit.*, p. ix.

50. Joseph, *op. cit.*, p. 5.

51. The Jesuit Volunteer Corps, for example, lists spirituality as one of its four core goals, together with social justice work, simplicity of life, and community. Recently, The Saint Vincent Pallotti Center for Apostolic Development in Washington, D.C., initiated a new publication *Shared Visions* to "assist in the spiritual formation of lay volunteers."

52. Joyce Hollyday, "Twenty Years under the Big Top," *Sojourners*, Vol. 20, No. 8, August-September, 1991, pp. 34-36 at 36.

Chapter Two

1. Amitai Etzioni, *Social Problems* (Englewood Cliffs, N.J.: Prentice-Hall, Inc., 1976), p. 173.

2. In many Mardi Gras organizations, discrimination against African-Americans, Jewish-Americans, Italian-Americans, and others has been traditional. These practices burst into the national news only in 1992 when the New Orleans City Council voted to bar discriminating organizations from the use of city facilities and certain services, and thus opened up pandora's box of debates, threats, and turmoil not yet resolved.

3. Joe Holland and Peter Henriot, S.J., *op. cit.*, p. 14.

4. Francisco Ivern, *op. cit.*, p. 19.

5. *Instruction on Certain Aspects of the "Theology of Liberation,"* Sacred Congregation for the Doctrine of the Faith, August 6, 1984 (Washington, D.C.: United States Catholic Conference, Publication No. 935), p. 17.

6. Thomas E. Clarke, S.J., "Methodology," in *The Context of Our Ministries: Working Papers* (Washington, D.C.: Jesuit Conference, 1981), pp. 6-9, at p. 7.

7. *Ibid.*

8. Joseph Daoust, *op. cit.*, p. 18.

9. Peter Marchetti, S.J., in an address to New Orleans Province Jesuits, December, 1979.

10. Pope Paul VI, *On Evangelization in the Modern World,* 1975, No. 20.

11. Joseph Daoust, *op. cit.*, pp. 8-9.

12. Christine Gaylor and Annelle Fitzpatrick, *op. cit.*, p. 7.

13. Joe Holland and Peter Henriot, S.J., *op. cit.*, p. 20.

14. *Ibid.*

15. Fred Kammer, S.J., *op. cit.*, pp. 150-151.

16. Marion K. Sanders, *The Professional Radical: Conversations with Saul Alinsky* (New York: Harper & Row, 1970), pp. 56-57.

17. More comprehensive resources exist for social analysis. I recommend the Center of Concern's *Social Analysis: Linking Faith and Justice* by Joe Holland and Peter Henriot, S.J., *op. cit.* Many of their approaches are reflected in this chapter, and they provide specific tools for beginning analysis. The respective human sciences—sociology, economics, political science, history, anthropology—have a wealth of approaches to social reality.

18. *Ibid.,* p. 28.

19. Marion K. Sanders, *op. cit.*, p. 50.

20. Amitai Etzioni, *op. cit.*, pp. 45-46.

21. Joe Holland and Peter Henriot, S.J., *op. cit.*, pp. 31-45.

22. Monika K. Hellwig, "Christology and Attitudes toward Social Structures," in *Above Every Name: The Lordship of Christ and Social Systems* (Ramsey, New Jersey: Paulist Press, 1980), pp. 13-34, at 19.

23. Cf. Amitai Etzioni, *op. cit.*, p. 2.

24. St. Ignatius of Loyola, *Spiritual Exercises.* In the rules for discernment of spirits, Ignatius suggests that the retreatant review the entire course or current of an experience in prayer or reflection: beginning, middle, and end. If the process of reflection misses the mark or ends badly, or is disturbing in going through it, then it is likely not to be graced. Beginning, middle, and end must all tend to the good. No. 333.

25. See, for example, the section on the structuring of reality in *Doing Faithjustice, op. cit.,* pp. 168-78.

26. Joe Holland and Peter Henriot, S.J., *op. cit.*, p. 14.

27. Amitai Etzioni, *op. cit.*, p. 114.

28. Catholic Charities/United Way Task Force, Msgr. R. David Cousineau, ed., *Catholic Charities and United Way: A Partnership for the Future* (Washington, D.C.: Catholic Charities USA, 1989), p. 5. This study raises important concerns

over structural change within United Ways and the changing role of United Ways.

29. *Ibid.*, p. 22.

30. Eugene Fontinell, "In Defense of Institutions," in *America*, Vol. 116, No. 9, March 4, 1967, pp. 314-316 at 314.

31. Donal Dorr, *Spirituality and Justice* (Maryknoll, N.Y.: Orbis Books, 1984), p. 59.

32. *Ibid.*

33. James A. Donahue, "The Social Theology of John Paul II and His Understanding of Social Institutions," *Social Thought*, Vol. 13, No. 2/3, Spring-Summer 1987, pp. 20-33, at 28.

34. Michael J. Maiello, "Modeling Organizational Culture in Catholic Social Services," in *Social Thought*, Vol. 17, No. 1, 1991, pp. 3-11, at 4.

35. *Ibid.*, p. 7.

36. Walter Wink, *Naming the Powers: The Language of Power in the New Testament* (Philadelphia: Fortress Press, 1984), p. 5.

37. Bill Kellermann, "Spirits of the Age: Walter Wink's Unmasking of the Powers," in *Sojourners*, Vol. 17, No. 5, May 1988, pp. 22-25 at 25.

38. Joe Holland and Peter Henriot, S.J., *op. cit.*, p. 26.

39. Amitai Etzioni, *op. cit.*, p. 117.

40. These connections were brought home to me in college by an important book from the 1950s about "Regional City" (later revealed to be Atlanta). The author's systematic inquiry into community decision-making revealed that the major community decisions, whether political, economic, or social, in Regional City were made by 40 men: 37 businessmen, 2 doctors, and one lawyer. No elected officials. A similar decision-making elite existed in the minority black community as well. Floyd Hunter, *Community Power Structure: A Study of Decision Makers* (Chapel Hill, NC: University of North Carolina Press, 1953).

41. Joe Holland and Peter Henriot, S.J., op. cit., pp. 26-28.

42. Nicholas Lemann, "The Unfinished War" (Part Two), *The Atlantic Monthly*, Vol. 263, No. 1, January 1989, pp. 53-68 at 68.

43. Joseph P. Daoust, S.J., "Economy," in *The Context of Our Ministries: Working Papers*, op. cit., pp. 30-35, at 30.

44. *Ibid.*, pp. 30-31.

45. Amitai Etzioni, *op. cit.*, p. 146.

46. *Ibid.*

47. Marion K. Sanders, *op. cit.*, p. 75.

48. *Ibid.*, p. 48.

49. Peter J. Henriot, S.J., "Social Analysis: One Year Later," in *Center Focus*, Issue 45, September 1981, pp. 2-3 at 3.

50. Francisco Ivern, S.J., "Socio-Cultural Analysis: How?" in *Promotio Justitiae*, No. 37, April 1988, p. 10.

51. *Ibid.*

52. Joe Holland and Peter Henriot, S.J., *op. cit.*, p. 92.

53. Kathleen M. O'Connor, "Wisdom Literature, Women's Culture and

Peace: A Hermeneutical Reflection," in *Blessed Are the Peacemakers* (Mahwah, N.J.: Paulist Press, 1989), Anthony J. Tambasco, editor, pp. 40-61 at 40.

54. Cf. Etzioni's analysis of how our prisons are actually creating the opposite results from their intended purposes. Amitai Etzioni, *op. cit.*, pp. 104-105.

55. Donald L. Gelpi, S.J., "The Converting Jesuit," in *Studies in the Spirituality of Jesuits*, Vol. 18, No. 1, January 1986, p. 26.

56. Donal Dorr, *Option for the Poor: A Hundred Years of Vatican Social Teaching* (Maryknoll, N.Y.: Orbis Books, 1983), pp. 108-109.

57. Maria Riley, O.P., "Women Workers in the Global Factory," in *Center Focus*, Issue 52, January 1983, pp. 3-4 at 4.

58. Donald L. Gelpi, S.J., *op. cit.*, p. 29.

59. Gerard A. Vanderhaar, *Christians and Nonviolence in the Nuclear Age* (Mystic, Ct: Twenty-third Publications, 1982), pp. 92-93.

60. Cf. discussion of unmasking the injustices lurking behind legitimized social structures. Fred Kammer, S.J., *op. cit.*, pp. 182-183.

61. Joe Holland, *Flag, Faith, & Family* (Washington, D.C.: Center of Concern, 1979).

62. Amitai Etzioni, *op. cit.*, p. 138.

63. *Ibid.*, p. 155.

64. Introduction, *Justice in the World*, Synod of Bishops, Rome 1971.

Chapter Three

1. Alfred C. Kammer, "On Justice, Community, Prayer, and Sundry Things," unpublished manuscript of Fall, 1981 dialogue of Jesuit National Social Ministries Board, p. 42.

2. Professor Robert Michael Franklin writes of his approach to social ethics in which divinity students are invited to share "your first experience of discovering racial and cultural difference" and how "your attitudes, perceptions, and behaviors" have developed since those experiences. It engenders "significant private talk," Franklin writes. "People tell their stories, often with a passion which suggests that they've waited long for the opportunity." It gives rise to elements of confession, conversation, cooperation, and criticism.

> I am persuaded that racism is so deeply woven into the fabric of Western consciousness that mere intellectual treatments of it are, at best, ineffectual. Bolder and riskier strategies of unraveling and disclosure are (morally) required here.

"The Case for Social Ethics," in *Theological Education*, Vol. 26, No. 1, Autumn 1989, pp. 43-61 at 55-56.

> 3. The aim of theological reflection may be described as the mediation of Christian vision, values and principles to the world of our experience objectivized through social analysis. It takes place in a kind of circular movement between past and present for the sake of the future, that is, between the heritage of primordial and perennial Christian experience and, on the

other hand, the "signs of the times," through which God makes himself
known in the events and experiences of today.
Thomas E. Clarke, S.J., "Methodology," *op. cit.*, p. 8.

4. "It is also, as in the case of social analysis, to accent the responsibility of
each Christian, with help from professional theologians and guidance from
the bishops, to speak the discerning word of faith in concrete historical situations." *Ibid.*

5. Michael H. Crosby, O.F.M., *op. cit.*, p. 147.

6. However, I find to my consternation, that call is not gripping enough to
   change me or to enlarge the scope of my practical concerns. It asks that I
   have a passionate desire to help in the achievement of justice for people
   in places, cultures, economic and social situations that I do not know,
   have no deeply experienced affinity with, and will probably never understand. I do not have that desire. Expositions of the call to engage leave me
   inert. There is something monumental, superhuman, about this struggle
   the Church and the Society [of Jesus] call us to engage in. The call over-
   whelms me, and I would rather not read or talk about it. [Bill Connolly
   letter to Phil Land.]

Bill Connolly, S.J., and Phil Land, S.J., "Jesuit Spiritualities and the Struggle
for Social Justice," in *Studies in the Spirituality of Jesuits*, Vol. 9, No. 4,
September 1977, p. 204.

7. Rosine Hammett and Loughlin Sofield, ST., *Inside Christian Community*
(Jesuit Educational Center for Human Development, 1981), pp. 16-17.

8. Dean Brackley, S.J., "Downward Mobility: Social Implications of St.
Ignatius' Two Standards," in *Studies in the Spirituality of Jesuits*, Vol. 20, No. 1,
January 1988, p. 25.

9. *Ibid.*, pp. 17-18.

10. Ruth Leger Sivard, *World Military Expenditures*, 1979 (Leesburg, VA:
World Priorities, 1979).

11. Dean Brackley, S.J., *op. cit.*, p 24.

12. Cf. John Francis Kavanaugh, S.J., *Following Christ in a Consumer Society*
(Maryknoll, N.Y.: Orbis Books, 1981), pp. 3-48.

13. Dean Brackley, S.J., *op. cit.*, p. 21.

14. John Francis Kavanaugh, S.J., *op. cit.*

15. Donna J. Markham, O.P., "Communal Life and the Global Reality," in
Human Development, Vol. 8, No. 3, Fall 1987, pp. 14-19, at 16.

16. *Ibid.*, pp. 16-17.

17. *Ibid.*, p. 18.

18. *Ibid.*, p. 19.

19. Rosine Hammett and Loughlin Sofield, M.S.B.T., *op. cit.*, p. 17.

20. Deborah Prothrow-Stith, "Deadly Consequences: Stopping Youth
Violence," *Connections*, Winter, 1992-93, pp. 6-8.

21. *Ibid.*, p. 21.

22. Hammett and Sofield stress helping members work through termination
and not insulate themselves from the pain. Groups must (1) complete unfinished business, (2) relive and remember positive group experiences, (3) inte-

grate what they have received from the group by reflection and sharing, and (4) describe and constructively express their feelings about termination. Finally, all terminations should be ritualized, grieved, and celebrated. *Ibid.*, pp. 26-27.

   23. This anguish brings an "unbearable pain" (p. 17), since it is the ache of our hearts for what we most need and want: to be loved. Deep within us this ache eventually becomes "division... fear... fragility... flight from pain... a defense system" (pp. 17-18). And because living close to our hearts means living close to our anguish, "contact with the deepest feelings of the heart is often an almost unbearable experience." We learn to build barriers around our hearts to keep away the pain. Cut off in this way from our hearts' feelings, we find ways to escape the pain. We use addictions to work, chemicals, people, sex to compensate for our unmet needs (pp. 47, 14).

Mary Ann Fatula (writing of Jean Vanier's book *Man and Woman He Made Them*), "Good News to the Poor," in *Spirituality Today*, Vol. 41, No. 4, Winter 1989, pp. 359-367 at 363.

   24. This would be similar to Pope John Paul's stress on "the desire for profit" and "the thirst for power" as the twin sources of social structural evil. Cf. *The Church's Social Concern* (1987).

   25. I hope to show that the very effort to live responsibly in one's interpersonal dealings with others must with moral inevitability fail in some significant measure unless one simultaneously attempts to ensure the responsibility of the decisions that shape human institutional living. In other words, only socio-political conversion can ensure the complete authenticity of personal conversion.

Donald L. Gelpi, S.J., *op. cit.*, p. 6.

   26. Alfred C. Kammer, S.J., "On Justice, Community, Prayer, and Sundry Things," *op. cit.*, pp. 38-39.

   27. Roger Haight, S.J., "Foundational Issues in Jesuit Spirituality," in *Studies in the Spirituality of Jesuits*, Vol. 19, No. 4, September 1987, pp. 1-61, at 42.

   28. Alfred C. Kammer, S.J., *op. cit.*, p. 48.

   29. John F. Kavanaugh, S.J., *On Small Communities and Living Among the Poor* (Washington, D.C.: National Board of Jesuit Social Ministries, 1981), p. 15.

   30. Donald Gelpi, S.J., writes, "We are attempting to prove that anyone who attempts to live a personally converted life without passing to socio-political conversion must inevitably succumb to some measure of irresponsibility in interpersonal dealings with others." *op. cit.*, p. 24.

   31. U.S. Catholic Bishops, *Economic Justice for All* (1986), No. 40.

   32. Thomas E. Clarke, S.J., *Above Every Name, op. cit.*, p. 3.

   33. Our analysis reveals also the limitations on moving through the Pastoral Circle inherent in the structures of some religious communities. In these, isolation, consumption, exploitation, and control seem to characterize much of the community's lifestyle, underwritten by a myth of apostolic efficiency. That myth holds that community is primarily a place to fill up the gas tanks for apostolic life on the road.

   34. Robert Michael Franklin, *op. cit.*, p. 57.

Chapter Four

1. Patricia Natali, Social Action Director of the Catholic Diocese of Newark, unpublished and untitled reflection paper, distributed by The Roundtable (an association of diocesan social action directors), 1988, p. 3, acknowledging influence in this part of Robert McAfee Brown's *Spirituality and Liberation* (Pa: Westminster Press, 1988).

2. James E. Hug, S.J., ed., *Communities, Social Action, and Theological Reflection* (Ramsey, N.J.: Paulist Press, 1983), p. 288.

3. Cf., for example, Albert J. Fritsch, S.J., *The Contrasumers: A Citizen's Guide to Resource Conservation* (New York: Praeger, 1974); John Haughey, S.J., *The Holy Use of Money: Personal Finances in Light of Christian Faith* (Garden City, NY: Doubleday, 1986); John F. Kavanaugh, S.J., *Faces of Poverty, Faces of Christ* (New York: Orbis, 1991).

4. James McGinnis, *Journey into Compassion* (Bloomington, IN: Meyer-Stone Books, 1989), p. 63.

5. *Ibid.*, p. 65.

6. *Ibid.*, p. 66.

7. Dean Brackley, S.J., *op. cit.*, p. 30.

8. McGinnis stresses the importance of **family** decision-making about lifestyle. James McGinnis, *op. cit.*, p. 72.

9. Robert Bolt, *A Man for All Seasons* (New York: Vintage Books, 1962), p. 66.

10. If we look at history from below, we hear in the Christian message first of all God's judgment on the world. For people caught in oppression, the Gospel is first of all affirmation; but for people associated with the dominant culture—such as we are—the Gospel is judgment before it offers new life. It is only after we have mourned, after the way of negation, that the joyful language of God's gracious presence recovers its true and authentic meaning....Mourning and lamentation become a permanent element in the worship of God.

Gregory Baum, *Compassion and Solidarity: The Church for Others* (New York and Mahwah, NJ: Paulist Press, 1990), pp. 87-88.

11. Beth Ann Corr, "Expectations, Heartbreak and the Relish of Small Victories," *Journeys and Dreams*, Vol. 15, No. 3, Summer 1992, p. 3.

12. Joseph H. Biltz, "Reflection on a Theology of Social Action," in *Charities USA*, Vol. 14, No. 3, April 1987, pp. 6-9, at 9.

13. Thomas Merton, letter to James Forest, February 21, 1966, in *The Hidden Ground of Love*, ed. William H. Shannon (New York; Farrar, Straus, Giroux, 1985), p. 294.

14. Wilfred L. Pilette, M.D., "Two Houses Fallen," *Human Development*, Vol. 12, No. 3, Fall 1991, pp. 36-38, at 38.

15. Peter J. Henriot, S.J., "Lessons of Seventeen Years...," *Center Focus*, Issue 88, January 1989, p. 6.

16. Harry Fagan, "Ten Points for Effective Diocesan Social Action Offices," *Origins*, Vol. 12, No. 42, March 31, 1983, pp. 672-76, at 676.

17. David Hollenbach, S.J., *Justice, Peace, & Human Rights* (New York, N.Y.: The Crossroad Publishing Co., 1988), p. 220.

18. Henri J. M. Nouwen, *In the Name of Jesus* (New York, N.Y.: The Crossroad Publishing Co., 1989), pp. 67-68.

19. Miriam Theresa MacGillis distributed by Christine Doby in 1988 *Roundtable* mailing.

20. Henri J. M. Nouwen, in Robert Durback, ed., *Seeds of Hope* (New York, N.Y.: Bantam Books, 1989), p. 170.

21. Henri J. M. Nouwen, "A Spirituality of Peacemaking-Part III: Saying a Humble, Compassionate, & Joyful 'Yes' to Life," *New Oxford Review*, Vol. 52, No. 9, November 1985, pp. 19-26, at 20.

22. Henri J. M. Nouwen, in Robert Durback, *op. cit.*, p. 176.

23. Roger Haight, *op. cit.*, p. 42, quoted more fully in chapter three.

24. Cf. Henri J. Nouwen, "A Spirituality of Peacemaking," Parts I-III, *New Oxford Review*, Vol. 52, Nos. 7-9, September-November 1985.

25. William L. Newell, "The Reflection Groups," in James E. Hug, S.J., *op. cit.*, at 57-58.

26. *Ibid.*, p. 43.

27. Thomas H. Groome, *Christian Religious Education* (San Francisco, CA: Harper and Row, 1980), p. 190.

28. *Ibid.*, p. 191.

29. Larry L. Rasmussen, "Community Reflection," in Hug, *op. cit.*, pp. 261-278 at 262.

30. *Ibid.*, p. 263.

31. Henri J. M. Nouwen in Robert Durback, *op. cit.*, p. 201.

32. Mary Ann Fatula, O.P., *op. cit.*, p. 360.

33. Christine Gaylor, C.S.J., and Annelle Fitzpatrick, C.S.J., *op. cit.*, p. 11.

34. John C. Haughey, S.J., "The Role of Prayer in Action/Reflection Groups," in Hug, *op. cit.*, pp. 103-121 at 110.

35. Larry L. Rasmussen, *op. cit.*, p. 277.

36. Patricia Natali, *op. cit.*, p. 9.

37. *Ibid.*

38. Henri J. M. Nouwen in Robert Durback, *op. cit.*, pp. 171-172.

39. Peter-Hans Kolvenbach, S.J., "Our Mission Today and Tomorrow," in *Faith Doing Justice: Proceedings of the June 1991 Conference* (Washington, D.C.: Center of Concern, 1992), pp. 44-53, at 52.

40. Roland J. Faley, T.O.R., "Leviticus," in *The Jerome Biblical Commentary* (Englewood Cliffs, NJ: Prentice-Hall, 1968), No. 7, p. 69.

41. Edward J. Mally, S.J., "The Gospel According to Mark," in *Ibid.*, No. 59, pp. 21-61 at 44.

42. James McGinnis, *op. cit.*, p. 129.

43. John C. Haughey, S.J., *op. cit.*, p. 107.

44. John Haughey, *Ibid.*, p. 113.

45. Henri Nouwen, "Discipleship and Reconciliation," *Pax Christi USA*, Vol. 16, No. 4, Winter 1991, pp. 20-21, at 21.

46. Henri J. M. Nouwen, "Compassion: The Core of Spiritual Leadership," *Worship*, Vol. 51, No. 1, January, 1977, pp. 11-23, at 21.

47. *Ibid.*, pp. 21-22.

48. *Ibid.*, p. 23.

49. David Hollenbach, S.J., *op. cit.*, p. 224.

INDEX